THE ORDER

To Andy,

Stay true to your path!

SCOTT STEIN

THE ORDER

Doing the right things,
at the right time, in the right way

Published by Vision Learning
PO Box 408, Freshwater NSW 2096 Australia
www.scottstein.com.au

First Published July 2015
Reprint November 2015

CiP details are available from the National Library of Australia.

ISBN 978-0-646-94164-6

Cover design by Dan Gregory, Impossible Institute
Edited by Russell Thomson, clearcommunications.net.au
Typsetting by Peter Guo, letterspaced.com.au
Printed by Griffin Press, Australia

CONTENTS

Acknowledgements

The writing of a book and passing on of knowledge and insights does not occur on its own. There have been many lessons and people who have inspired me on my journey to stay true to my path.

To my wonderful wife, Natalie, I want to thank you for all your inspiration and encouragement. I still love your energy, your passion and your zest for life and this has only grown since the day we met. I look forward to our next date night and many more adventures together.

To my incredible children, Jasmine, Isabella and Luca, thank you for being the great kids that you are. Jazzy, your wonderful smile always lights up a room and reminds me to show love. Bella, your passion and commitment to push yourself to new heights inspires me. Luca, your cheeky laughter and wonderful hugs remind me to have more fun.

I would also like to thank my parents, Larry and Lorene, for inspiring me to educate my mind, explore the world and feed my soul. Also to the numerous mentors who have taught me and shared their wisdom. Bruce, thanks for sharing your infectious energy and your friendship. Bud, thanks for being there and reminding me of the path. David, thanks for giving me the chance to be an adventure guide. Aunt Irene, thanks for showing unconditional love. Uncle Bob, thanks for stretching my mind and my thinking.

To Tom Brown and Stalking Wolf and the many elders who have guided me, my greatest respect and admiration for passing on the ways of the past so we can use them today to guide us toward a better future.

To Helen Macdonald for being a wonderful business partner for over 15 years (longer than many people are married!) and The Learning difference team for helping us lift performance for so many people and organizations over the past 15 years

To Matt Church, thanks for being a thought leader, mentor and business partner and helping me to stick to my path. The Thought Leaders tribe would not exist without you. To Michael Henderson thanks for the talks, insights and encouragement along the way. To Pete, Christina, Ral, Mel, PK, Neen and the rest of the Thought Leaders Global tribe, thank you for your support and brilliance.

Thank you Peter Baines for your vision and offer to get involved with Hands Across the Water and board members Kay, Willie, and Scott for making a difference to our Thai children, staff and their communities.

I would also like to thank the amazing Katrina Welch. As my business manager you keep me organized, make incredible things happen behind the scenes and can switch directions at a moment's notice (sorry!). Thank you for your patience, friendship and commitment.

I would also thank you for following your intuition and picking up this book.

Introduction

I have written this book to address the deep need I have identified from a number of emerging patterns and trends. Many of these are not good – some things are so completely mixed up and out of order it is difficult to see how to get them back on track.

There are millions of disengaged people in the workplace who want to be stretched and to thrive at work. They want to be committed, motivated and active in achieving results and being part of something greater than themselves. They want leaders who inspire and involve them. Leaders they would walk over cut glass for. Unfortunately, too many leaders still use the ways of the past, are not able to adapt to changing needs and settle for short-term results for personal financial gain. Some leaders ignore what they know to be right and take what they can – they do not know how long their grasp on power will last.

There are a host of people in government and in our communities who recognize the need to help their fellow man. They want to build a society that cares for everyone, regardless of background, race or religion. We live in one of the most self-actualized timeframes in history – we desire to become everything we are capable of.

Unfortunately, we have politicians who look after their own interests, rather than the greater good. We have become disillusioned by government infighting and the protection of constituent power bases to the point that we do not trust any of the candidates.

Religious leaders take advantage of those whose faith they should encourage by indulging in mental, physical and sexual abuse. Celebrities and sporting stars use community and charity organizations to funnel their income to family and friends. They use tax loopholes to their own personal advantage and trick us into believing they are doing the right thing.

At home, the struggle to keep up with work means less time to focus on family and friends – those we believe the most important to us. Often children are being raised by strangers because their parents need to work, are separated or simply caught up in their own lives.

Many schools use teaching methods that are stuck in the past century. They do not harness the potential of our young people or prepare them for jobs and businesses that may not even have been thought of yet. Thankfully, there is still hope and increasing pressure to ensure education meets the needs of the current world.

On a personal level, we are so busy we do not have the time to meet or get to know our neighbours except when we see them putting out the trash. We keep the doors locked, the curtains drawn and stay in the protected patch we call home. Driving through our community, we keep a wary and suspicious eye on anyone we do not recognize for fear something bad could happen. We know we should do more, but we do not have the time. We are overwhelmed by all the things we have to do – we are just too busy.

Why is everyone so busy? What are the life-threatening, world-shattering things filling our time and head space so that we miss the important things in life? How do we change the distorted reality that is starting to shape society and influence future generations?

We need to get back to what is real and find a way to reconnect with our soul, to listen to the voice deep inside that lets us know what we should be doing and how we should be doing it.

We have to rediscover what I call the critical path. We need to retrain ourselves to follow an internal hierarchy of how to get things done – one that is based on belief, commitment and the search for the positive potential in the people and the opportunities around us.

Our critical path is shaped primarily by how we do things. This does not just mean deciding on the need to take action and do things differently. Specifically, it is how we do these things and the strategies we can use to make sure this order is the right order.

Am I on my Critical Path? Five Simple Questions

These five key questions can be used to assess if you are on your critical path. They appear to be quite simple and unassuming, but be warned, these questions have powerful intent and are designed to stir the soul. Use them to reflect and connect and decide if you are currently doing the right things, at the right time and in the right way.

Question #1: Are you doing what you should be doing with your time, energy and commitment?

This is a broad question that asks you point blank if you are on path. It is relevant for both work and home. The answer should be a clear and confident yes or no. Anything in between is just an excuse or justification for why you choose not to do the things you know you should. If you can't answer yes, you need to ask more questions and seek more answers.

Question #2: Is there a better way to do things and a smarter order to do them in?

Again, this can be at work or at home. This question asks you to analyse how you have been behaving and the sequence you have been taking. Are you harnessing the potential of your people at work? In a conscious way? Are you making time to let your family know they are the most important people in your life? We are so often caught up in our busyness we are not even aware of the order we do things in. By taking a few moments to reflect, we can either be content or start considering alternatives.

Question #3: What is stopping me from doing what I should be doing in the way I should be doing it?

This is designed to look directly at obstacles that may be stopping you from reaching your true potential, to consider the distractions and fears that take you away from your true path. It can also be quite confronting as it requires you to take a hard look at yourself and recognize your limitations or the patterns of behaviour that get in the way. However, without identifying what is blocking your path, you may never see it.

Question #4: If I were to start doing the things I should be doing, what could happen?

By looking at the brightness of the future we can begin to see new possibilities. We are often limited by our past experiences. We can only see the immediate future – generally a very narrow focus. There is an endless realm of future possibilities we need to embrace. By opening up to alternatives, we can look beyond the 'here and now' and rekindle our dreams, both long lost or newly created.

Question #5: If I were to die tomorrow, would my family, friends and work colleagues say that I had lived a life to be admired?

This is not for the faint hearted. It is one of the most crucial and confronting questions we should ask ourselves. We have a finite amount of time to do the things we are meant to do and we cannot afford to continually put off deciding what our critical path or destiny should be. 'Today is a good day to die' is a famous Native American saying that was quoted to author John Neihardt in the 1930s by Oglala Lakota Medicine Man, Black Elk. Although there are different interpretations, I believe it makes you ask on your death bed if you would be truly fulfilled by the life you have lived. If you don't think you would, what do you need to change or do differently to get your order right?

These questions are simple and it is easy to rush a response or fake an answer. However, your intuition may start questioning whether or not you are being true to yourself and true to others. Once this happens, you will generally remind yourself that there are other things you should be doing as they become more apparent.

The purpose of this book is to provide a signpost for you to start thinking about what you are doing. I am a Pathfinder, someone who can see the way ahead and whose purpose is to guide others to walk their critical path.

Initially, I worked with youth and community groups to help them to connect with themselves at a deeper level. As well as mainstream youth groups this also included stints working with young people who were behaviourally challenged and considered dangerous to society. By changing their environment and taking them away from the temptations and distractions that filled their world, I noticed a deep shift in their energy and their mindset. Many emerged from living behind a tough façade to wanting a better life.

Working with community leaders, university students and teachers allowed me to see how the not-for-profit sector operated, to see brilliant examples of innovation and ways to create and achieve results without the financial resources of the business world.

For over 25 years I have worked in the business world with literally thousands of people across various industries to help them identify and head towards their critical path. This has ranged from senior-level strategic planning to front-line manager development on how to approach their staff in a way that improves and sustains their performance. This has taken me across geographical borders and into numerous locations from boardrooms to shop floors. I have often taken people away from the distractions of their technology to the wilderness to provide them with a chance to reconnect with what is real.

Most leaders seem to know what they should be doing, they just forget how to do it and get busy doing things that do not matter. Many have been conditioned to hold on to too many things and not delegate and empower those beneath them to step up to the next level. I have also seen the incredible energy that can fill an organization when their people gain momentum on their critical path and start getting their order right. The passion, commitment and achievements of many have been inspiring and a shining example for others to follow.

My wish is that the messages in this book become a positive ripple in people's minds. That this ripple spreads out and starts to influence people to step up and start courageously walking their critical path. More importantly, I want to show others what leadership truly looks like, regardless of whether it is at work or at home. Then we will get our order and priorities back on path. We will start doing the right things, at the right time, in the right way.

Section 1

What Is Taking People Off Path?

What is it that is stopping people from doing the things that they should be doing? What is it that gets in the way of good intentions and the conscious desire to achieve our goals? It is simple common sense to realise that there are things we need to do at work that are crucial to achieve results.

The challenge is that Common Sense is not Common Practice. We do not always do what we know we should. For example, we know that for better health and wellbeing we should drink seven to ten glasses of water a day, eat three to five pieces of fruit and vegetables and exercise at least four times per week for 30–45minutes. This is common sense. The question is 'have you done this consistently every day and every week?'

We know we should do all of these things, however, when looking back over the past couple of weeks, many people would have to admit that they have not kept up these activities consistently. There are a number of reasons that arise to stop people from doing what they know they should be doing, but when asked why, the biggest excuse is: 'I did not have enough time.'

It is as if there is simply not enough time for people to get the things done that they want to. This is a worrying trend. It is leading to many people just going through the motions to try to keep up. If you ask what they are trying to keep up with, you would get a range of responses. Most would say they feel they can't get things done or are unable to stay on top of all the tasks they need to do.

So why is everyone so busy? What are the life-threatening, world-shattering things that are filling up their time and headspace? Good question, isn't it? Many people just 'pretend' that they are very busy doing important things. However, when you ask them to step back and analyse their activities, those things start to look more trivial and unimportant.

It is as if people have forgotten how to prioritise what matters. If you ask them to write down what the most important things in their life are, you would get a list of higher order items such as spouse, kids, family friends, health etc. However, if you then ask them to list what they have been focusing their time and energy on over the past couple of weeks, most people would list work activities, trivial tasks and other time-fillers.

For many people there is a gap between what they want to achieve and their reality. This is starting to cost us as a society. It is taking its toll through increasing stress leave at work and increasing rates of anxiety and mental illness. It is also starting to affect future generations as they experience the impacts of this gap. In addition, the younger generation is being brainwashed at a faster rate than ever before into the rampant consumerism fuelling this frenzy of activity to keep up.

The Pathways of Distraction: Five Trends

Looking at the current landscape, there are a number of emerging patterns and trends, but many people are busy or on mental autopilot, they are not aware of them. They are busy being active doing tasks that may not be serving them – or the companies they work for. It is challenging for them to be able to break out of the everyday routine to see what their common patterns or habits are. Few have the ability to see these patterns while they are involved in them. It is an unconscious cycle that keeps them on the treadmill, completely unaware as life passes them by.

Others are aware of some of these trends. They can hear the voice in the back of their mind that lets them know that there is a better way of operating – they just choose to ignore it. They may keep themselves busy with activities so they can insulate themselves from the need to take immediate action and convince themselves they will get around to doing things differently later on.

By understanding these trends and patterns we can make a conscious choice to start doing the things that we know we should be doing. We can be more effective and have a more positive impact on the work that we do and on the people we do it with. Specifically, there are five broad trends that are occurring that keep people from doing the things that they need to do. These trends are limiting our potential and our capability at work and at home – we need to examine them.

Chapter 1

Trend #1: Digital Overload – We can't keep up

How do I keep up with all the information that arrives in my inbox? I clear it and five minutes later another 10 emails come in. It is not uncommon for someone to have a 'to do' list that is never completed. The list continues to grow and more things are identified that need to be read, researched, decided or completed.

For many people this creates a sense that they are drowning in information and there is no end in sight. The need to keep up is constant and the treadmill not only continues to spin, it is speeding up and people need to run to keep up.

Did you know?

The pace of change has accelerated. The access to and amount of data now being shared is phenomenal – it is unequalled in human history.

- In 2014 almost 5,000 books a day were published worldwide (UNESCO). If you look at only the English Language books, this is reduced to 1530 books a day. To be able to read all of the books published today you would need to read one book a day for the next five years.

- There are over 40,000 Google searches per second – that is over 3.5 billion searches a day! You can spend hours just searching for things. Over 300 hours of video are uploaded to YouTube every minute – all ready to steal your time and entertain you with dancing cats and other frivolous clips.
- More data and information has been created in the past five years than in the past 100 years – and it is growing!
- New generation fibre-optic technology will have the ability to carry 10 trillion bits of information per second down a single strand – a capacity for 150 million phone calls every second.
- In 1910 the 10 largest businesses in the world were involved with constructing and selling products large enough for humans to stand on. In 2010 the largest businesses were predominately associated with the creation and sale of the invisible, intangible and the handheld.
- 79% of Smartphone owners check their device within 15 minutes of waking up.

This is the new world we live in. Gone are the days when we could manage the pace and speed of new information. In the workplaces of the past, there was not as much information arriving at the same time. The immediate sense of urgency to respond to communications was minimal because the flow of information coming across one's desk was manageable.

Annual Google Searches 1999-2012

Google now processes over 40,000 search queries every second on average (visualize them here), which translates to over **3.5 billion searches per day** and **1.2 trillion searches per year** worldwide. The chart below shows the number of searches per year throughout Google's history:

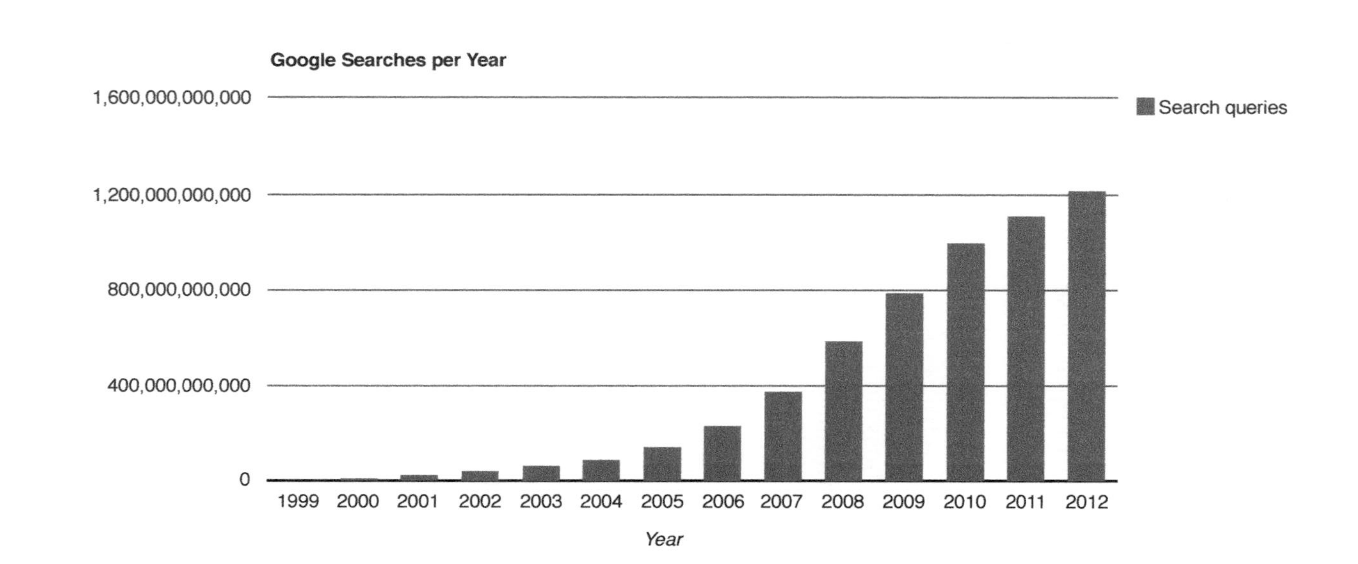

Graphic Source: Google

Remember when?

In the 1980s and 1990s the communication of information in the workforce was confined to the physical world. If someone wanted to share information or get you to make a decision they could send a letter through the post or use internal mail. You could wait to open these items until you were ready (or until the mailroom person brought them around). If it was more important they would call your telephone extension which was physically attached to your desk. This meant that if you were not there, or busy doing something else, voicemail would capture their communication.

If you wanted to get new information or gather new insights there were not a lot of places to look. If you wanted to find out the latest data, you only had a limited number of sources that you could go to. These were generally confined to four broad categories: books, periodicals, magazines and the traditional media.

Books have been a longstanding source of information. The challenge was in the methods available to find out which books were worth reading to provide the information you were looking for. One of the most popular methods of identifying books worth reading was from *The New York Times* Best Seller list. Published since 1932, this list is based on actual sales of books from booksellers across the United States. You would, however, have to wait for the weekly list to be printed then buy a newspaper to read it.

The other method of searching for books was to go to a library. Trying to explain what a card catalogue system is to the younger generation is challenging. For those who grew up in this era, you will remember a large wooden box full of drawers, containing thousands of paper index cards showing the title, author and the decimal reference code of the book. Each index card would have to be read individually to identify a book that may be of interest. You could not remove the card from the drawer. You needed to write the details down and then set off across the library in search of the book.

Using the decimal code you would look up and down the library shelves reading numbers and glancing at titles. Having located the book you would need to see if it really was of interest or not. Often you would find that the book had been checked out by someone else, sending you back to the card catalogue system to find an alternative!

You needed to subscribe to magazines and research articles to get the latest copy – or go to a library. These were generally published monthly and if you missed an issue it would be challenging to find out what was in it because there was no simple database you could use to search through past issues.

Traditional media meant newspapers, radio and television. Most people would get a daily update. from reading the newspaper (often in the morning over breakfast), listening to the news on the radio or from the evening news report on television. These were the primary methods of keeping up with current events on a local, national and international level. They were confined in time and could easily be managed by putting down the paper or turning off the radio or television.

Information was also confined by geographical boundaries. There was easy access to news of local events and this was where most focused their attention. National and global matters were not given as much time or space in the media.

Approach to marketing

The approach to marketing and advertising of products and services has also changed significantly. In the past most businesses focused on advertising in the physical world, i.e. in print, in an attempt to generate sales.

One trusted source of marketing that every business had to be in was the Yellow Pages. This was one of the first static databases that provided a listing of the details of businesses and the services they offered. Looking for a plumber? You only had to flip through the pages and find numerous pages of plumbing businesses with their phone numbers. Some businesses would also pay more for larger display advertisements that showed the services they offered and increased the size of their phone number encouraging people to call them. This large book of yellow pages was provided to all households and businesses free of charge once a year. This was often the 'go to' source of advertising as it was simple to find the contact information.

Other forms of marketing were also popular, but again they were physical items and almost exclusively paper based. Businesses would do mail-outs in an attempt to grab attention or to promote items for sale. For this form of advertising to have an impact, you needed to personally receive it. This created special 'mail houses' that produced and distributed marketing material via direct mail. One of the early powerhouses in this field was Michigan-based Valassis Communications Incorporated. Valassis started as a printing house producing newspaper mail-outs and flyers and grew to become a multibillion dollar global company that developed targeted direct-mail databases for businesses. While this was the most effective way of marketing in the past, the shift to the digital world since the 90s has seen it decline significantly.

Cold calling in person or trying to generate business over the phone was also very simple in nature. It involved just one person finding the phone number for a business (usually from a telephone book) and calling the switchboard to identify the appropriate department or person to speak to. If you got past the switchboard, you would find many managers would have an assistant to act as a 'gatekeeper' and limit access (those were the days!). This is very different from the automated and digital approaches that have started to take hold across business and society in the 21st century.

The new millennium

A significant increase in digital communication has occurred after 2000. Companies now have established websites and developed digital marketing campaigns. Databases can be programmed to send information and marketing promotions without human intervention slowing the process. Better yet, the cost of producing and distributing this information is significantly cheaper than in the old days of printing a brochure and posting it to customers.

This new technology means email inboxes are now constantly full of information. The Radicati Group is a marketing research company that has been tracking this information since the very early days of the internet. Their 2014 'Email Statistics Report' highlights this worrying trend. According to their report they have found that email will continue to grow from just over 4 billion accounts to over 5 billion accounts by the end of 2018. The business world consumes the majority of these emails with over 108 billion sent and received each day. On average, business users send 121 emails a day with this expected to increase to 140 emails per day by 2018.

Imagine what it would have been like writing and opening over 100 letters a day in the 1980s and 90s. People did not have the time (or the technology) to allow them to respond to this amount of information. If they had tried, they would not have had the time to complete the job they were being paid to do.

The Information super highway

So what has allowed this to happen – and in such a short space of time? How did we go from a business world with manageable information and communication levels to one that bombards us with so much information that we cannot keep up? In a word: technology. Specifically, technology that is speeding up the creation and dissemination of information.

Initially the internet was set up to allow access to, and sharing of, information. The purpose was to use the digital world to find any information that was required. However, from the early days the internet has gone through some significant changes.

In the 1960s, the concept and initial design of the internet was led by the US Defense Advanced Research Projects Agency (DARPA). The military had a specific interest in using this as a way to increase (and encrypt) messages that could be sent between locations. According to the Internet Society, some time around 1985 the early form of the internet was split between the MILNET (for military use) and ARPANET that was used by research organizations and universities. From there it was further enhanced as a result of the push for a US National Research Network in the late 80s and early 90s and evolved into the World Wide Web by MIT's Laboratory for Computer Science professor Tim Berners-Lee and Al Vezza.

Internet Speeds 1993 vs 2014

	1993	2014	Future
Speed	56kps	1.5-5mbps	100mbps
Time to download single song	10 minutes-high speed 30 minutes-low speed	4-5 seconds	under 1 second
Time to download full length movie	28 hours-high speed 3 days-low speed	18-24 minutes	7-8 minutes

Source: Akamai Technologies 2014 State of Internet Report

The speed of the internet has increased significantly. In the days of ARPANET the processing speed was 50kbps and dial-up internet access over telephone lines to the World Wide Web was limited to 56kbps in 1993. This meant that it took 10 minutes at full speed (or 30 minutes at low speed) to download a single song. A full-length movie would have taken 28 hours at full speed (and up to three days at low speed!).

Broadband is a term that refers to connections faster than dial-up. Although this was available to a select few in 1996, it did not become mainstream until the mid-2000s. The speed was initially 1.5 to 5 Mbps and has increased further as technology has improved. This now means a single song takes 4–5 seconds to download and a full-length movie 18–24 minutes (of course, now you can watch the movie via streaming while it is being downloaded!).

The new fourth generation (commonly referred to as 4G) technology has the capability of reaching speeds over 100Mbps. According to Akamai Technologies 2014 State of the Internet Report, mobile device connectivity is also increasing with speeds reaching over 100Mbps. This means downloading a full-length movie will be reduced to 7–8 minutes.

What this means to mere mortals

This increase in the speed of delivery of information is starting to overwhelm people as they try to keep up. Although speed and access to information has increased, our brain's mental capacity has remained the same – our ability to read and process data and to take action is much the same as it was 20–30 years ago. This has created a vast disconnect in our ability to keep up and is having a negative impact on us both mentally and physically.

How often in the past week have you had the thought that it feels like there are not enough hours in the day to finish everything you need to do? This is becoming the new norm, the accepted way of being in our new 24/7 lifestyle. It is spreading like a plague as we pass the need to operate at warp speed on to the next generation.

The rapid speed of information is starting to desensitise many workers to the constant barrage of data. They are recognizing that they cannot keep up and are switching to mental autopilot. They get overloaded with information and after a while cannot effectively identify what information is important to read and take action on versus information that is simply filling their headspace.

Research into the brain is revealing the negative impact of this overload. In his book *Activate Your Brain: How understanding your brain can improve your work – and your life*, Scott Halford says that the perceived threat when we are confronted with too much information can shut down the brain. Specifically, with overstimulation and intensity of information, the brain becomes disorganized and cannot process all of the information coming in at the same time. As a result the prefrontal cortex, the part of our brain responsible for reason, analysis, innovation and managing emotion, stalls due to brain chemistry and natural reactions to stress being overwhelmed. One of the most significant findings was around perceived dangers such as looming deadlines. Our brain magnifies the negative potential and both adrenaline and cortisol are released. This can often lead to creating a foggy mind, which can impair our thinking and by default our activity.

Business have also felt this impact. The pressure to keep up that employees are feeling has never been higher than it is today. Trying to stay on top of all the communication and possible options to consider is occupying more and more time – which means less time for people to focus on what their role requires them to do. There is more information to be understood, less time to do it and the list of tasks that need to be completed gets longer. There is also not the additional full-time support available to help struggling employees as budget controls keep costs to a minimum in the attempt to stay competitive. So many staff get the feeling that they just need to suck it up and keep their heads above water for as long as possible.

So what do they do? Many give up. They go through the motions, looking busy, knowing that they do not have a chance. They want to keep their job so they do the best they can. This often leads to the creation of additional electronic files and emails to indicate that they have been busy. The importance of these emails may be minimal, but they provide evidence of activity so that they feel more protected in their roles if anyone wants to see what they have been doing.

Managers can't keep up

This information overload has created an additional challenge for managers. Staff drowning in data has a knock-on effect across functions and departments. The stress to keep up and maintain performance is fierce. Performance targets have not been adjusted so that managers can allow their staff more time to deal with these new complexities, which has resulted in many managers also working more hours in the push to keep up.

The increase in unused holiday leave demonstrates the impact on managers and their staff. Many of them do not take time off because their teams are stretched too thin and they do not have the people or resources to cover their absence. This is reflected in the increasing amount of annual leave that is being accrued globally. Expedia's '2013 Annual Vacation Deprivation Report' states that, on average, workers do not take five days of their leave entitlement each year. The biggest reasons cited are economic conditions and trouble coordinating friends and family. While this figure included both staff and management, many managers take less of their holiday time given they have overall responsibility (and accountability) for departmental targets being reached.

In addition, managers are being challenged to find ways to continually motivate and inspire staff who feel the burden of information overload. Finding new ways to recharge batteries and keep people feeling balanced at work is becoming more and more common.

Few managers have the skillset, or have been trained in how to keep themselves and their staff on top of things in this new, challenging environment. For many, even taking time out to invest in being trained in these skills can be challenging due to the increased workload. Using the internet to develop these skills has also had mixed success. Sorting through the thousands of online learning platforms and the millions of informational videos consumes so much time that many managers do not use them.

The digital world continues to grow. More data and more content are being uploaded daily. Keeping up with the digital overload feeds into the next trend, the inability to focus and manage distractions.

Chapter 2

Trend #2: Distraction Management – Lack of focus

Focusing on what is important is becoming harder. With the constant barrage of digital information and an overabundance of consumer choices, people are not focusing on what matters. They are being distracted by things that are not relevant or important. It is estimated that, on average, we have 4,000 thoughts per day flying in and out of our minds. This makes it extremely challenging for us to be able to focus on any one thought for any period of time before another one pops up to distract us.

The need to start focusing is becoming so relevant that a number of best-selling books have come onto the market that specifically deal with the need to focus. Well-known authors now see the need to focus as one of the most important issues facing today's society.

In Daniel Goleman's latest book, *Focus: The hidden driver of excellence*, he calls this the era of unstoppable distractions and argues we must learn to sharpen focus if we are to contend with, let alone thrive in, a complex world.

The creators of the 50 million books sold worldwide in the 'Chicken Soup for the Soul' series, Jack Canfield, Mark Victor Hansen and Les Hewitt, have published a book in this area: *The Power of Focus: How to hit your business, personal and financial targets with confidence and certainty.*

In addition, a search on Amazon.com will display 100 pages of books that feature the topic of 'focus'.

Not only is there more information to focus on, but the constant access to it from numerous sources, including the mobile devices that we keep on our person 24/7, exacerbates the problem as does the limitations of our brain as revealed by neuroscience.

How the mobile device has taken control

The popularity of mobile computing devices now means that we cannot escape being 'wired in' to the constant stream of digital data. Increased internet speeds means the ability to stream information and video to mobile platforms is now commonplace.

When Apple launched the iPhone in 2007 they did more than bring a new product to the market. They completely transformed and revolutionized the entire mobile phone industry. Before Apple introduced this incredible device, we were all satisfied with the mobile phone. The ability to make and receive calls while out and about was great. The likes of Nokia, Blackberry and Motorola dominated the mobile phone industry and were considered untouchable giants. Their phones were also starting to allow emails to be sent and received, and consumers put up with the slow speed and non-graphical interface.

The iPhone was a breakthrough internet communications device – a true smart phone. It not only turned the mobile phone industry upside down, it also introduced consumers to a product that allowed them to do more than just make calls and send clunky emails. The touchscreen that immediately responded to provide multiple items at once, quickly showed that this was a new device that would take us to the next level. It is hard to imagine what it was like before 2007 without this device. Back then you had no Google Maps, no integrated calendar, no ability to Face Time from your mobile phone, no web browser to search the internet and no App Store to provide every type of software program imaginable. Of course, now the market is flooded with these smart phone devices that put the world at our fingertips. It is interesting to note that Blackberry, Nokia and Motorola are now small players or out of the mobile phone market – a massive shift in less than 10 years!

What does the mobile device allow you to do? Basically everything. The list of functions is exhausting – all of the many things that can steal your time and distract you from what is important at work and at home. We now keep our mobile device with us at all times. In fact, many people sleep with the mobile phone next to their bed, which can also lead to more distractions and interrupted sleep as they ding or buzz as new messages come in at all hours.

Walk into any restaurant and you will see people on their mobile devices. It is not uncommon to watch a family with both parents and all of their children on a tablet or mobile phone checking email, Facebook or any number of other things to pass the time.

Households now have an abundance of these mobile devices to keep people plugged in whenever they want 24/7. The 'Ericsson North America Mobility Report' published in June 2015 shows how prevalent these devices are in our world. As of 2014, 90% of US households have three or more internet connected devices, and just under 50% have five or more devices. The study also reports that 64% of the North American population use the internet everywhere, including indoors, outdoors and in vehicles.

In Australia the population is even more plugged in. According to eBay and Telsyte's 'The Economics of Electronics Report' from June 2015, Australians now have on average of eight internet connected devices. This includes an average of two computers per household, more than 1.5 smartphones, a printer, a tablet and a games console. It is predicted that by the year 2020, 90% of the world's population over six years old will have a mobile phone, with the majority having access to the internet.

The impact of speed

With the increase in internet speeds, the mobile device is now able to offer more ways to distract people. As previously mentioned, digital data transmission has steadily increased from the early days of the internet. Now the speed of this data transfer has truly taken hold of us.

What this means is that the small handheld devices that we

take with us everywhere from the bedroom to the bathroom are now wired in to provide even more distractions 24/7.

According to the Australian Bureau of Statistics there was a 33% increase in downloads over the 12 months from 2013 to 2014. This shows the voracious appetite we have for getting access to information whenever we want it.

Now over 50% of YouTube videos are being downloaded onto mobile devices. This means that what was traditionally confined to a stationary computer is now being taken with us everywhere. Stuck on a bus or train for 15 minutes, you can now wirelessly stream videos on your mobile. Take time during your lunchbreak to check your Facebook status and you will be able to auto play the numerous videos that are embedded in posts to help you pass the time.

In other words, it is now even harder not to be distracted because of the constant physical reminder of the digital world.

How social media and non-work-related websites steal our time

In addition to all the work tasks that we have to perform and the daily emails we need to respond to, what else is distracting us? Social media and non-work-related websites. Today there are hundreds if not thousands of these sites with the most popular being Twitter, Instagram, LinkedIn. The biggest one of all is Facebook.

Facebook was not the first social media site that allowed people to connect online – a number of these sites were operational before Facebook started in 2004. What Facebook did was create a platform that enhanced the user experience. It not only allowed us to easily post information (including photos and video), it let us know when our friends posted information.

It is a great social tool that allows people to find out about friends and family located across the globe. The brilliance of the coding allows users to upload photos and videos, as well as join communities and promote products and services (including games) to their friends. It is not difficult to spend hours reading what your friends and family are doing based on their posts on Facebook.

More importantly, Facebook is designed to create such a positive experience that we want to stay connected. Nir Eyal is an IT consultant who helps companies find ways to create habit-forming products that change user behaviour to keep them engaged. In his book *Hooked: How to build habit-forming products*, Eyal describes one of the most important tools to get people hooked is what he calls 'triggers', which involve a series of touchpoints to remind the user to get involved by creating habitual patterns. A common trigger is getting a user to invite other users (think of the 'Friends you may know' section on Facebook). When we engage with these triggers it creates a pyramid-style framework that grows significantly in a short time. Daily users create activity (think tagging, posting, etc.) that gets other users to respond and perpetuates the cycle further for others to take notice.

This means people are constantly being reminded of what their friends are doing – and encourages them to respond. This becomes a habit that keeps people wanting to stay up to date and not miss what their friends are posting – which, of course, distracts them from focusing on what they should be focused on. When was the last time you caught yourself going onto Facebook just to check your newsfeed?

So how much time are people wasting on Facebook and other social media websites? *Forbes Magazine* found that 64% of employees visit non-work-related websites each day. They also reported that over 60% of those admitted to wasting at least one hour per day on these websites with Facebook contributing to over 50% of this time loss. How much is this costing business? Billions. Take a look at the table below that shows the cost per employee due to this lost time and productivity.

Dollar Value of Lost Productivity	
Number of working days per year (take out 4 weeks annual leave and 2 weeks public holidays)	250 days
Number of working hours per day	8 hours
Number of working hours per year	2000 hours
Lost hours per day due to non work related websites	1 hour
Lost hours per week	5 hours
Lost hours per month	22 hours
Lost hours per year	264 hours
Average Salary (Australia)	$74,725
Average Salary per hour (Australia)	$37
Average Dollar Value Lost–per employee	
per day	$37
per week	$187
per month	$822
per year	$9,864

The rise of mobile devices and social media websites has created one of the largest distractions we have. Another main distraction is the number of decisions we need to make and the endless choices that confront us on a daily basis.

Distracted by choice

All of the revolutions in the internet world, both physical and digital, are not the real distraction. The real distraction is the unending access to multiple choices that these platforms offer. The human mind works best when it has a manageable number of decisions to make at any given time.

When we are provided with too many choices, too many options at the same time, it starts to overwhelm our brain. Multiple choices become multiple distractions and make it harder for us to focus on what is really important.

One of the best descriptions of this new challenge is provided by American psychologist Professor Barry Schwartz in his book *The Paradox of Choice: Why more is less.* Schwartz points to the out-of-control consumerism and number of choices that now control our lives. He provides some incredible examples that we as consumers are faced with every day, including dealing with supermarket shelves that hold more than 30,000 items. Schwartz also looked at the time that can be lost when shopping around between products because there are so many to choose from.

The paradox that Schwartz identifies is that the majority of people want freedom of choice to select what they want when they want it. The challenge is that the majority of people also want to simplify their life – to make things easier. Sadly, the more options available, the harder it is for people to make an easy decision. What he also points out is that with the increase in options, come three distinct consequences: (1) decisions require more effort; (2) the chance of making a mistake increases; and (3) the psychological consequences of making these mistakes are more severe.

Limitations of our brain

Neuroscientists agree that the decision-making network in our brain is not always effective and does not prioritise when it is overloaded. This means that we are even more open to distractions as new interruptions and information start overloading our brain. Our brains do have the ability to process this information, it just makes it more challenging to sort the trivial from the important information, which takes energy and can increase frustration.

In *The Organised Mind: Thinking straight in the age of information overload*, Daniel Levitin looks at the processing capacity of the conscious mind. It is believed that physiologically we have the ability to process 120 bits per second of information. It takes 60 bits of information per second for us to understand a person talking to us. This makes it very challenging for our brains to process information if another person is talking to us at the same time. As Levitin describes it, the challenge is that the bandwidth in our mind limits the amount of information that we can pay conscious attention to.

So how does our brain cope with more information than it can effectively manage? It either blocks it out – or it continually changes focus from one bit of information or interruption to another. Whether it be the buzzing of your mobile phone in your pocket informing you of a new email or the overwhelming number of choices that you need to make daily, all are distracting us from focusing on what is important. Worse yet, many of us believe that being this plugged in is the new norm.

Chapter 3

Trend #3: The Busy Syndrome – Gotta be busy

We now have a belief that if we are not busy doing something, we are wasting our time. It is as if society has become so highly strung that we need to be constantly occupied. And worse yet, it does not matter what it is we are doing – as long as we are busy at it.

This is 'The Busy Syndrome', a widely held belief that we need to be busy all the time. It is the myth that, by being mentally and physically active, we are moving in the right direction – and accomplishing more.

In the 1970s and 80s many people had a bucket list – a list of things that they wanted to do before they died. Often it would include three to four big items that they hoped they would be able to do one day. This may have included a big overseas trip to somewhere they always wanted to visit, seeing their children married and finally paying off their mortgage and being debt free.

Now the number of items on the bucket list has changed. No longer is it sufficient to have three or four items – many people have up to 100 items on their list. This rush to experience all that life has to offer is linked to the psyche of people who feel they need to get busy or they'll miss out.

Across the workplace everyone will tell you they are very busy. The list of tasks to be accomplished continues to grow and people feel the pressure to keep up. Because of this they convince themselves (and others) that they are busy. But what are they busy doing? The '2015 Australian Future Leaders Index' created by BDO and the Co-op identifies this new culture of busyness. It describes it as a modern-day phenomenon within developed societies where individuals have a sense of having too much to do, being overcommitted, constantly rushed and possibly overwhelmed as a result.

Their research shows that 65% of these future leaders aged 18–29 feel busy either all the time, very often or quite often. Even more interesting is that 61% of those surveyed like being very busy. The report also brings in social commentator Tim Kreider's views that busyness is a personal choice and that many people are addicted to busyness because they dread what they may have to face in its absence.

Are people keeping busy just so they do not have to think about life when they are not busy? Are the tasks that they are busily doing really important? Many people are just going through the motions, filling their time with activity so they can appear to be busy.

This results in people not doing what they should be doing. Many are not aware that there are other things that they could (or should) be doing because they are so busy that they cannot stop to get perspective. They are stuck on an endless treadmill that is not leading anywhere.

This is fast becoming an epidemic that it is impacting on the next generation. Not wanting their children to miss out on any opportunity, parents are encouraging their kids to get involved in everything. Gone are the days when a child could play one or two sports while at school. Now they are involved in numerous activities outside the classroom. It is not uncommon for a child to participate in five or six different extracurricular activities each week. They play soccer, attend dance classes, practise with a gymnastics squad, take swimming lessons and learn a musical instrument. Parents are now spending more and more of their time driving their children to and from events so they can cram in as many activities as possible.

The phrase 'Tiger Mother' was coined by Amy Chua in her book *Battle Hymn of the Tiger Mother*. This showed the growing trend of Asian mothers to push their children to achieve more through a very strict and disciplined approach that filled their children's day with scheduled events to increase their chances of gaining a place at a leading university. These Tiger Mothers are not interested in their children playing and having fun. Research into this approach has shown that it can increase a child's grade point average and opportunity to gain one of the competitive spots at universities. It also found that these students were more likely to have more self-image issues, more conflicted relationships with their parents and the expectation to be successful makes the achievement of success less satisfactory or fulfilling.

The parents are passing their need to be busy on to their children.

Busyness addiction and biochemistry

Human beings have natural psychological and biological habits or addictions, and being busy is one of them. We get a buzz out of getting things done – regardless of the importance of the activity – and this often becomes an addictive response that we crave.

Every time we complete a task or send an email, we naturally feel a sense of accomplishment. However, we know that there is more to this. Our brain's biochemistry also triggers a hormone that reinforces this behaviour. Dopamine is one of the key neurotransmitters and is linked to addiction.

In a way, doing trivial tasks becomes a way of self-medicating, allowing us to feel a sense of accomplishment. In a famous experiment completed in the mid-1950s, brain researchers Peter Milner and James Olds placed small electrodes in the brains of rats to stimulate that part of the brain that released dopamine when they pressed a lever in their cage. The rats became so addicted to this stimulation that they eventually ignored everything else – including food. They continued to press the lever – up to 700 times an hour – until many of them collapsed or died from exhaustion or starvation.

This is not only confined to animals. There are now reports that a man in Guangzhou, China, died after playing video games continuously for days. The Daxing Internet Addiction

Treatment Centre in Beijing was started in 2006 and has treated over 6,000 people for addiction. Zigor Aldama visited the facility in 2015 and wrote about it in an article in *The (UK) Telegraph.* The centre's leading psychologist, Tao Ran, believes that internet addiction leads to problems in the brain similar to those that occur with heroin addiction.

So we are wired to get immediate stimulus for any activity that gives us a sense of accomplishment. For many this addictive state has become their everyday mode of operating. They are stuck in the myth that being busy is good, so they continue not to do the things that they should be doing – or not doing them in the order they should be done.

In the workplace this means that people are constantly interrupting their workflow so they can complete small, trivial tasks to gain a sense of accomplishment. This breaks their concentration, which, in turn, limits their productivity as they constantly check their inbox for the next stimulus.

Chapter 4

Trend #4: Lack of Awareness

Another reason why people are not doing the things that they should be doing is that they are not aware. They do not realise that there is another way to do things, another approach that could help them achieve more and be more fulfilled.

Why? Many people are living their lives on autopilot. They have their awareness set on cruise control because it is easy and comfortable. As humans we develop patterns of behaviour that become habits, which keep us stuck in a particular way of operating.

Think about your routine. What is the sequence of activity you follow every morning from the time you wake? In reviewing what we do day in and day out we recognize that we are creatures of habit. The way we brush our teeth, fix breakfast and drive to work remains largely the same.

One of the challenges of this habitual approach is lack of awareness. Have you ever arrived somewhere you drive to on a regular basis and not been able to remember the drive? You don't remember passing a particular school or landmark along the way. More than likely you were on autopilot. You did not have to consciously think about what you were doing – you had done it so many times before, it had become habitual.

Pulitzer Prize-winning author Charles Duhigg provides a simple way to understand how habits form. In his book *The Power of Habit: Why we do what we do in life and business*, he looks at a three-step process called The Habit Loop. The first step is when a trigger or cue sends your brain onto automatic selection to determine which habit is to be used. The second step he describes is when it becomes physical or mental routine. The final step he describes is a reward system that allows your brain to determine if the loop is worth embedding into memory. As this loop continues through these three steps, he found that the initial trigger or cue and the reward become interconnected and this results in a natural anticipation or craving that occurs.

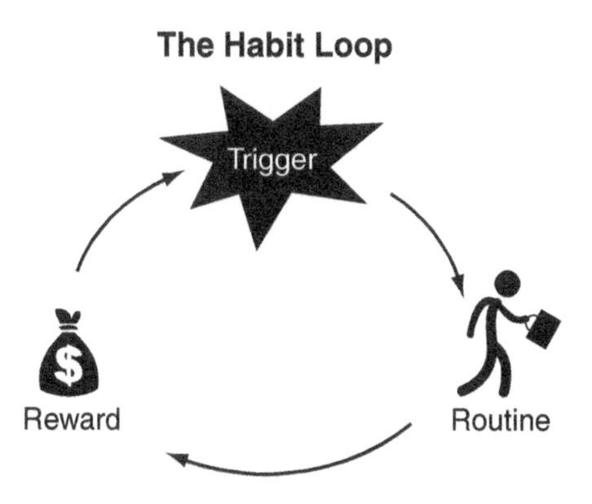

There is a common saying that 'Ignorance is bliss'. This is true because when we are not aware that there are alternatives, it makes life simple. The lack of awareness of other options or choices means that we do not have to waste brain power and energy considering alternatives.

The habitual patterns we create keep us from seeing new options we could be taking. Some of these are small, insignificant things while others are more important things that we should be aware of. We constantly need to increase our awareness.

Do you know of someone who is not happy in their job? You can see that they could be doing something else that would allow them to reach their potential and be fulfilled. Often the challenge is that they are stuck in a job and are unable to see the possibilities available to them. They are unaware of these and continue to suffer in a role that they are not suited for.

In the workplace

Many of us have worked with a colleague who has very low self-awareness. Often they are unaware of the way their behaviour and approach negatively impacts their performance – or the performance of others. They may have the best intentions, it is just that they mix up the sequence they take to get things done or fail to get others involved.

This is a common occurrence with managers and their staff. The leadership team decides to go on a corporate retreat to identify their vision and strategic plan. Upon returning to the workplace they tell the staff about the new direction and are surprised that many are not motivated. They missed a critical step: they did not get the staff involved in the decision-making process. Without this important step, leaders can actually turn people off.

Engagement Surveys that measure employee satisfaction highlight this problem. The '2013 Gallup State of the American Workplace Report' found that 70% of American workers are 'not engaged' or are 'actively disengaged' and emotionally disconnected from their workplace. The Report also estimates that these disengaged employees cost the US between $450 and $550 billion each year in lost productivity. The leading factors for this employee disengagement can be found in the relationship between the employee and their direct manager.

The business world invests millions in providing feedback to improve staff and managers' self-awareness. Just telling someone that they need to improve is generally not enough. Because many people lack the ability to be aware of their impact on others, companies have turned to statistical analysis to identify and measure current performance. Studies suggest that almost 30% of companies use some type of multi-source feedback with many using 360 degree feedback surveys, also known as multi-rater feedback. These surveys involve gathering feedback from subordinates, peers, and colleagues, which is designed to provide them with self-awareness about the approach they are using and how effective it is.

It is believed that this feedback increases performance because individuals can see and understand the specific areas where they need to improve – things that they may not have not been aware of. There is a range of empirical data that supports this, but there are also numerous studies that show people resisting this feedback. It is understandable that a manager who has been operating in a particular way for 20 years may react negatively to feedback that suggests there is another way of doing things – one that is perceived as more effective.

This feedback runs counter to how they have habitually operated, which, naturally makes it more challenging to accept and more challenging to change. The paradox is that we know that things change and we need to adjust to keep up with these changes yet we are more comfortable with our habitual approach and it takes more energy to change. For many, having to do things differently also raises a sense of fear and anxiety .

Chapter 5

Trend #5: Increase in Fear and Anxiety

Fear and anxiety provide another reason why people are not doing the things they should be doing. It is instinctual for us to protect ourselves from anything that makes us fearful. Human existence has flourished as a result of our ability to identify physical threats and ensure that we are safe from them. For an increasing number of people anxiety limits their ability to do what they should be doing.

With everything moving so much faster, we are becoming fearful of our ability to stay in front. The sound of a new email or post arriving on our mobile phone makes us alert. We need to check it, afraid that we may miss something and be left behind. As already mentioned, some people even sleep with their mobile phone next to them so the sound of emails arriving in the middle of the night disturbs their sleep and they scan to see if there is something that needs to be responded to.

The influence of negative news

With news media now plugged into our lives more than ever before, there is a constant stream of stories designed to grab our attention. Unfortunately, the most common headlines include any number of negative themes: natural disasters, riots and unrest due to shootings, murders and crimes – any number of frightening things.

It is as if we have programmed ourselves to look for negative news. Two researchers from McGill University in Canada, Marc Trussler and Stuart Soroka, conducted an experiment to understand how people filtered news information. They found that most people simply scanned the headlines and were more likely to recall negative stories rather than positive ones. They call this tendency to remember (and actively look for) bad news 'negativity bias'. Of course, this could be something hardwired into our primitive survival instincts. Our ability to identify dangerous things and move away from them is what has allowed the human race to thrive. It is unfortunate that news of dangerous things has become so common that many people feel the need to protect themselves.

This fear has become so prevalent in the United States that the number of concealed handgun permits has soared over the past decade. The number of Americans so fearful that they feel the need to carry a gun has gone from 2.7 million in 1999 to 11.1 million in 2014. The US National Instant Criminal Background Check System (NICS) also reports that the number of gun purchases doubled between 2006 and 2014.

So, on one hand, people want to live in a safe and supportive world that is full of opportunity, but at the same time they also recognize that there is danger and a need to keep themselves safe from threats – physical and mental. Maintaing this balance is challenging and takes time and energy as they continually listen to the positive and negative self-talk in their mind.

Cherokee Parable of Two Wolves

The Cherokee were one of the largest Native American tribes and one of the first to integrate with the early European settlers. They lived in the south-eastern part of what is now the United States and were one of the few Native American tribes to have their own written language. They are considered a highly spiritual tribe with many customs and stories passed from generation to generation.

One Cherokee story captures the challenge that we have in balancing the positive and negative voices in our heads that can take us off path. A Cherokee elder teaching his grandson tells him:

'There is a battle between two wolves that live inside us all. One is evil and filled with fear, jealousy, greed, anger and hatred. The other is good and filled with peace, love, faith and kindness.' Upon hearing this from his grandfather the grandson asked, 'Which wolf wins?' His grandfather simply replied, 'The one that you feed.'

The challenge for many people today is that they are feeding the fear. Anxiety and depression are now reaching all-time highs in the Western world. This is costing society billions of dollars in medical expenses, sick time and lost productivity. It is keeping people from doing the things they should be doing and making the difference they should be making.

A global issue

According to the 2015 Future Leaders Index, this unhealthy anxiety and stress is already having an impact on the next generation to enter the workforce. As we have stated, the Index tells us this generation is already showing early signs of burnout with 82% reporting they suffer one or more physical health issues when they get busy and 76% reporting one or more mind or emotional health issues when they get busy.

This is creating a global epidemic and is such a worrying trend that, in 2001, the World Health Organisation (WHO) gathered Health Ministers from around the world to examine these trends. The 'Call to Action Report' looked at upcoming health trends and predicted that Mental Health would be the second largest global disease facing the world by 2020. The WHO's global research also found that five of the 10 leading causes of disability worldwide are mental problems – including major depression, schizophrenia, bipolar disorder, alcohol use and obsessive–compulsive disorder. These disorders combined with anxiety and stress are already having a significant impact on the working population.

Anxiety impact in the workforce

When staff cannot focus or are stressed at work, it has a significant impact on business performance. An increase in anxiety leads to an increase in stress leave and absenteeism as workers cannot cope with the resultant physical and emotional consequences.

Safe Work Australia released a report on work-related mental stress and the cost to Australian business based on workers compensation claims. The loss of productivity due to stress leave costs $10 billion per year. Claims for mental stress are the most expensive form of workers compensation claim and more professionals are making such claims. This report is based on actual claims for compensation and support. It does not include the cost for overtime or additional resources to cover employees' absences. It is estimated that the real cost of stress is actually more than $30 billion a year.

Stress and anxiety is increasing because of the rate of change. Things are moving so much faster than in the past that many older employees believe they may be on borrowed time. They are constantly on the lookout for the next new innovation that could replace them. Whether this is a younger and mentally faster replacement or a new form of technology that automates their role, both are at the back of their mind. Everyone knows of someone who had a safe and secure job but was made redundant when the organization needed to take a new direction. This means that rather than focusing on what they should be doing, many employees are being distracted by this fear about their future. The lost productivity is costing businesses and also leads to a lack of fulfilment for many workers.

All of these trends are taking people off path. Overwhelming distractions limit their ability to get things done. There are things that can be implemented to change this pattern. There is an order people can impose to get things done and a way to ensure that they do this so that it works both for them and for others. The next section will look how to do this and the importance of making to this shift for ourselves and for future generations both at work and at home.

Section 2

How to Get Your Order Right

What do we need to do to get back on to our right path? What can we do to ensure that we are doing the things that matter, rather than getting sidetracked with trivial things? I know there have been times when I have been overloaded, overworked and needed to get back on track. Who hasn't – when the kids are saying that you missed their big game, your staff look at you as if you are missing something and the voice in your head is exhausted?

To stay on our critical path we need to make the decision to do the right things at the right time in the right way. We need to find a higher order of being and doing – something that is desperately needed in all walks of life.

The society that we live in is artificial. We get caught up with the consumerism, the busyness just to be doing something, and forget what is real. What's more, many people fill their minds with hours and hours of other people's thoughts. At first this came from reading books, but over time extended to radio and now many of us watch television, sitcoms in particular, to pass the time and fill the void we feel inside.

It is so easy, and comfortable, to watch the latest popular television show. Whether it's 'Game of Thrones' or one of the numerous reality television programs such as MasterChef, there is plenty on offer to fill time. How often have you come home from a long day at work and just wanted to sit down in front of the television (or nowadays an iPad) and mindlessly 'tune out' for a while.

You know there are other things you should be doing, but

you just don't feel like doing them. Or maybe your habit is to sit down and do nothing. You know keeping up with the next television program is not as important as other things, but you just don't have the energy.

Watching a screen is soothing to the brain – we do not have to engage our conscious mind, but can sit back and be taken on a journey that others have created for us.

Surprisingly, television is not being replaced by the internet. Research shows we are spending more time in front of both television and computer screens. According to a 2006 study by Jupiter Research, a large number of us watch television and surf the internet on computer screens. This research found that, every week, 42% of the most avid television watchers (35 or more hours per week) also spent 30 or more hours online.

Going online gives us easier access and unlimited viewing that can even be taken with us on mobile devices. How much time is wasted watching YouTube videos or on Facebook looking at what friends have been doing? Our intention is to just take a quick look but an hour can fly past without us being aware. The younger generation spend hours on the myriad of popular online games, such as Minecraft and Candy Crush that keeps them busy and distracted. For parents, one of the biggest challenges can be pulling their children away from these screens.

Our thoughts or others?

Too often we do not know how to create our own original thoughts because we are so used to listening to others. This creates an unhealthy pattern that is starting to make our ability to think clearly and identify the way forward more challenging. Research shows that the amount of obesity in the Western world is increasing as our society becomes more unhealthy. The Australian Government reports that, in 2015, 63% of adults are overweight or obese – an increase of 10% since 1995. Most of this is due to lack of exercise.

Our physical inactivity is only half the challenge. Mental inactivity is increasingly common across society. Many people are becoming mentally unfit because their minds are on autopilot as they unconsciously drift through life. Research reveals that we start to use our brain less when automation takes over and it starts to become lazy.

In *The Shallows: How the internet is changing the way we think, read and remember*, Nicholas Carr provides an extensive list of psychologists and neurologists who have been conducting research on the brain and how it operates. The neuroplasticity of the brain shows that when our brains are active, the cells in our brain grow bigger. Likewise when our brain is not actively used, our brains atrophy or start to waste away. Carr followed this with an article in *The Wall Street Journal* with an even more specific message – evidence shows that computer automation is starting to 'dumb us down' rather than making us more intelligent.

When we do not actively use our brains, we stop thinking, we stop creating and do not stay in a heightened level of awareness. This leads to us being more passive and losing focus and we end up not doing the things we should be doing because we are overly influenced by information coming from other places to replace our thoughts.

As a modern society we need to be aware of what is happening to our original thoughts. Without these we become lost as we forget to remember what is important to us and why we do the things we do. As the incidence of mental illness increases, we need to reconnect with what is important. We need to get people to go back to a life which is simpler and where it is easier to identify what our focus is. We need to start listening to ancient wisdom that has endured the test of time and coexisted with the invention of new technologies.

Ancient Wisdom

History shows there is plenty of wisdom that has been taught through the ages and passed on from one generation to the next. Throughout time, across the globe, there are pockets of brilliance and wisdom that have guided people.

This ancient wisdom can be gathered into a range of sources: philosophers, teachers, leaders, warriors and healers. Some of them have names that are recognizable from early Western civilisation such as Aristotle, Socrates and Plato. Others from the Middle East and Asia, also recognizable, hold a stronger spiritual nature, including Jesus, Confucius, Lao Tzu and Buddha. Their teachings and writings provide insight and wisdom.

Other ancient knowledge has been taught and passed on from generation to generation that does not have a hero figure or deity persona attached. This can be as simple as how to sooth a crying baby to how to track animals from their prints. These skills were passed on between generations – father to son and mother to daughter. Generally these teachings were directly linked to the natural world, to what was real and what could be shared without the need for complex thought, reams of data or technology. There was a sense of balance and coexistence with the world without the need for scientific evidence to explain and rationalise everything.

The Natural Order of Things

In life there is a natural order. Nature follows patterns and sequences that have been around since the beginning of time. We know that there are four seasons – spring, summer, autumn and winter – that are cyclical and constant. We do not question their order, in fact we know that they will occur and we organize our life around them.

We also have a natural order that we follow as a species. We are born, we grow into children, we become adults, we have children, we become old and then we die. The cycle of life is a natural sequence that we understand and do not question. We know there is a natural order our life will follow.

What if there was a natural sequence or an order we could use to help us to do the things we should be doing, rather than getting sidetracked by other things. That order would need to be adaptable so we could use it in any situation to help us stay on track and remind us of what is important. More than just a series of thoughts or a checklist, it would also need to be something that would allow us to connect with our soul and know that we are still on path.

More importantly, the approach would need to be something that has lasted through time, not the latest management fad or popular psychology being promoted to sell books. It would need to be contained in ancient wisdom that has lasted for thousands of years and that generations of people across the world have used to help them stay on path and help them survive over time. It would need to be a Sacred Order.

Chapter 1

The Sacred Order – Native people's order for survival

For centuries indigenous people around the world had to prioritise what was important for them to survive. Aboriginals in Australia, tribes in Africa and Native American Indians all used their instincts and their experience to ensure their existence. They followed a universal set of guidelines or rules that allowed them to survive in their environment – the Sacred Order. This was passed on from elders to children, from generation to generation long before we modernised the world in the late 1800s by controlling our environment artificially through the use of technology.

Simply put, the Sacred Order was a sequence followed to ensure survival in any given environment, which would change as the people travelled to different regions and when conditions changed with the seasons. The Sacred Order was the constant approach that guided them.

More importantly, it provided a hierarchy to be followed to ensure that people did the right thing in the right order at the right time. To ignore the order and sequence was to risk life and decrease survival prospects.

I first came across the Sacred Order when I was at university in my mid-20s. I grew up in Michigan where there were plenty of rivers, lakes and woods that provided me with a sense of adventure and kept drawing me back to the wilderness. This may have been instinctual as my great grandmother was a full-blood Cherokee medicine woman. Unfortunately, she married a white man from outside the tribe and was banished. None of the Cherokee history or traditions were passed down to my grandmother or my mother. I had a typical American middle-class upbringing – but was drawn to the wilderness and nature.

While at university I became an adventure guide during the summer break – canoeing, backpacking, white-water rafting, cycling and rock climbing. To help become a better guide I read every book I could get my hands on, including survival books. After guiding adventure trips for about five years I came across someone who would teach me the ways of the Native Americans. Tom Brown Jr was taught and mentored by an Apache elder called Stalking Wolf. From the age of eight to 18 Tom spent his afterschool hours, weekends and summer holidays learning the ancient Apache rituals and philosophies.

I remember sitting in the bush being taught about Native American wisdom and survival. I quickly realised that many of the things I had learnt from books were wrong and no match for what I would learn through first-hand experience. I was also taught about the Sacred Order.

The Sacred Order consists of four distinct levels of activity that provided a hierarchy of what to do and in what order when in a survival situation.

Sacred Order of Survival

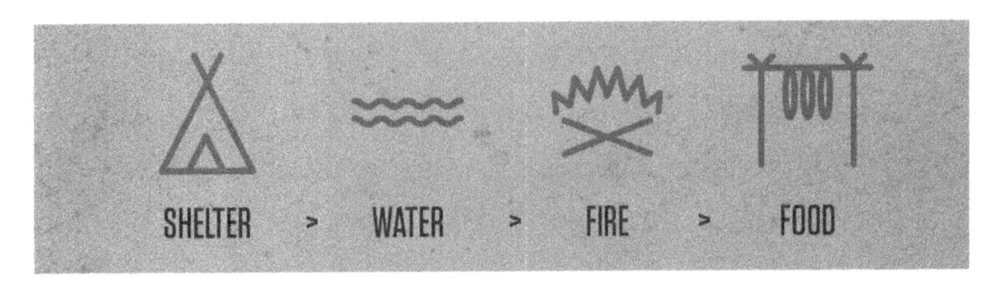

This simple yet powerful order allowed many generations of human beings to survive over time. It was simple enough for young children to remember and flexible enough to allow for instinct and intuition to be combined with intellect.

Shelter

This is the first thing that needs to be found in a survival situation. Exposure to the harshness of the elements can very quickly kill someone – within hours. Human bodies are fragile when it comes to dealing with extremes of temperature.

With rising temperatures, the human body starts to overheat. The body naturally starts to sweat to cool down, which in turn leads to dehydration. In the outdoors dehydration is a silent killer because it quickly impairs decision-making and judgement. Extreme dehydration starts to have a negative impact on bodily functions as internal organs begin to shut down.

With colder temperatures the human body also reacts to

protect the heat in the body's core. When the core temperature reaches a particular level, hypothermia sets in. Shivering, the unconscious muscle stimulation our system uses to try to increase temperature, stops and the brain starts to shut down. This eventually leads to a sleep-like coma that results in death.

The importance of shelter was taught by many different methods. Shelters were built of things that could easily be found in the region and suited the purpose of the people.

The North American tribes in the north built bark wigwams and lodges built of earth. In the south they built stone and adobe shelters and grass-thatched huts. The nomadic tribes in the plains region built teepees that could be moved as they followed the seasons and migrated for hunting. In the far north the Inuit people built snow igloos.

Indigenous people across the world built similar types of shelters. In Africa, they mainly built mud houses and straw huts. Australian Aborigines built bark houses as well as spinifex grass huts.

All shelters were built out of local materials that could be gathered easily. The kinds of shelters and the way they were built may have varied, but the importance and significance never waned – it was the highest priority of any village. When a tribe moved, it looked for the best place to build shelters, ensuring there were plenty of resources to help sustain them over time.

In harsh conditions people can quickly die within hours without proper shelter and protection from the environment. Shelter always remained the first priority.

Water

Water was the second priority in the Sacred Order. This makes complete sense given that half of our bodies consist of fluid. Without water we become dehydrated, which can lead to catastrophic consequences. Sources of water also need to be clean, not contaminated with parasites or harmful bacteria. Drinking polluted water can cause diarrhoea, which in a primitive setting can quickly lead to dehydration as the body cannot keep body fluid levels in equilibrium with physical needs.

Native people were taught various methods of finding clean, drinkable water. The most popular and easiest method was to gather water at its source, which could be a fresh spring coming out of the earth or by using a natural filter system to remove impurities. Some communities created sophisticated systems to filter water. One common method we all know today is to boil water to kill any bacteria. Of course, putting a pot of water on the stove was not an option in primitive times, so they would heat rocks in fires and drop them into water stored in carved wooden bowls.

Being without water for three days can impair thought processes and affect judgement. The longer we go without water, the more severe the impact on our system and the closer we come to death.

Fire

Fire is third in the Sacred Order, after shelter and water. We have a unique relationship with fire. Most of us can remember camping or sitting next to a fire that provided warmth and comfort, especially at night. For native people, fire was important because of its many uses.

Fire can be used to cook and warm food and liquids. In cold climates the warmth can help keep body temperature at the proper level, which reduces the caloric intake required to keep warm. In addition, cooking meat can kill the bacteria that may lead to a range of illnesses. Curing meat with heat and smoke allows it to last longer, rather than having to be eaten within days and reduces the risk of food poisoning.

Fire was also used to create tools necessary for survival. Timber spears were hardened in a fire to keep the tip from splintering when hunting game. Heat was used to shape and straighten wooden spears and arrows so they would fly straighter and more quietly. The hot coals were used to burn out bowls and the cooled-down ash was spread on warriors' bodies to mask their scent from prey.

Fire provided light that allowed native people to continue working or preparing food after dark. Today we forget how reliant we are on electricity to provide light. When the sun goes down, it can quickly become dark and that limits our activities due to the risks involved and the difficulty of completing complex tasks.

For many primitive tribes, a fire was also used as the place to gather. It was used in rituals and ceremonies that brought people together and helped strengthen their sense of connection. There is a psychologically soothing effect that can come from the warm embers of a fire. It has a calming effect that allows people to relax at a deeper soul level.

Food

The final priority in the Sacred Order is food. Many people mistakenly place food as a higher priority in the Sacred Order of survival. Just the thought of being stranded on a deserted island immediately makes us think, 'How long can I last without food?' Native people however understood that food is not the highest priority when it comes to survival.

Studies show us that we can go for weeks without food if necessary. Mahatma Gandhi, in his non-violent campaign for independence, survived 21 days on a hunger strike with only water. So, we can last longer without food, than we can without water.

Food for native people consisted primarily of either animals or plants. Animals were hunted on the land, in the sea/lakes/rivers and in the air. Hunting takes highly developed skills as well as tools to be successful. It also requires a large amount of energy to be expended as one moves to track, locate and hunt the prey. In primitive times, hunters had to ensure the energy used in the hunt was not greater than the energy gained from the animal food.

Plants provided a range of edible food, such as vegetables and fruits. Different seeds and plant material could also be ground and mixed to create other kinds of food. Grinding corn into flour allowed for the making of breads that could be stored and eaten over time. However, the identification and selection of plants that were edible and not poisonous was a critical skill. Eating a toxic vegetable, such as a poisonous mushroom, had disastrous effects.

Without grocery stores stocked with food, people had to go days and often weeks without food. This could also have been due to lack of hunting success or a sudden seasonal change in weather conditions with snow covering the fruits and vegetables. As we all know, food is still important and going without can result in illness, starvation and death.

This Sacred Order to survival provided native people with a way to make decisions and prioritise what was most important and what needed to occur next. It made things simple and could be adapted to manage any environment.

The Order is something that we can use today. If we can employ a simple and memorable approach to making the right decisions in the right order, we can ensure that we are doing the things that matter, without getting sidetracked by things that are out of order.

Chapter 2

Ancient Wisdom for Modern Times

The wisdom of the ages has been passed on through generations. There is a truth need to start tapping into to help us deal with the fast pace and many challenges of modern times. By looking backward we can learn strategies to use today.

Much of the ancient wisdom has already been blended into our business culture without our being aware of it. There is a range of ancient philosophies and terminologies that we use every day without appreciating their significance or how they lasted through time to the present day. Some of these include:

Chief Executive Officer. This title has been integrated into almost every large company or organization around the world. They are the highest ranking leader and have overall authority and responsibility for the organization they lead. The first word says it all. Native American tribes were led by a Chief who was responsible for protecting the people and culture. In addition, they carried the responsibility of sharing wisdom that was passed down through time. It is interesting how this has carried over into the business world and remained.

Tribe. For native people their tribe was more than a label to describe them, it provided a sense of identity – who they were as a people. It was an interconnected group of people living together following a similar culture or set of beliefs. One of the world's leading anthropologists on culture and business tribes, Michael Henderson, captured the description of a tribe perfectly in his book *Get Tribal: Simple, sound advice for understanding and improving your workplace culture.*

Tribes use their culture to safeguard themselves against change and simultaneously they also use the strength of their culture to effectively embrace new ways of thinking and working to ensure the culture adapts to changing times and circumstances.

On the war path. This was a common phrase used to describe the situation when Native Americans had committed themselves to warfare with other tribes or people. These native warriors were considered to be fierce – a force to be admired and feared. In today's language it is often used with more negative connotations. People know to avoid someone if they are on the war path and stay out of their way.

Bury the hatchet. This is a phrase that is used to signify that an agreement of peace has been made. It is commonly used to encourage people to set their differences aside and reach a common resolution. For Native Americans, when a peace was reached between tribes, they would both participate in a ceremony where they each buried a tomahawk in the ground to signify that their friendship was re-established.

In addition to those common phrases that have been integrated into our everyday language, there is other ancient wisdom that we can use to help us get our order right. To help learn from this ancient wisdom and approach there are three strategies that can be used, which involve listening to oneself and tapping in to the wisdom of others to stay on path.

Strategy 1: Track the signs

The first strategy that you can use to get back on path and ensure that you are doing the right things in the right order is to be aware of what you are currently doing. This is more than just taking a minute to look up over your computer screen and having a thought about what the 'to do' task is for the day. It requires you to take a clear look at what you are doing based on previous activity – not based on previous intention.

Many people have the best of intentions and have wonderful dreams and desires, however they do not know how to bring them about. They are caught in 'The Busy Syndrome' and are often not aware the actions they are taking are frivolous and not helping them stay on path.

To start changing this situation they need to start tracking their past behaviour and look for the signs they are leaving behind. For people to start tracking themselves, they need to start looking at things differently. They need to stop operating on autopilot and start taking a look at what they are doing by reviewing the 'prints' that they are leaving behind.

The reputation of native trackers is legendary. Whether

they are Aboriginal trackers in the Australian Outback or the legendary Apache scouts found in the South-western part of the United States, both are revered for their skills. They have the ability to easily and quickly identify tracks or signs of activity that the untrained eye does not see. This can be as simple as a print in the sand or the pattern of prints that show the speed, mindset and health of an animal.

In addition to teaching me and others about Native American Survival and wisdom, Tom Brown Jr is also one of the most well-known trackers in the United States. He gained his reputation as 'the tracker' because, by his late 20s, he had successfully tracked hundreds of people who had become lost in the wilderness. In his book, *The Science and Art of Tracking*, Brown talks about the signs a tracker can see that others cannot. In looking at the signs an animal has left behind, he believes that the master trackers actually become the animal and connect on a spiritual level to what they were doing at the time.

As someone who has studied with Tom, I know it is truly amazing what you can see in a footprint when you have been taught. I remember the first day I studied tracking with Tom. After providing an overview of how to read a track, he took me and the other students to an area in our camp that was full of prints. He bent down and started analysing a human footprint. He described the speed and the direction the person was heading in and quickly deduced that they were male.

Tom then looked at smaller things in the print and informed us that the person's stomach and bladder were full. He also pointed out that they had an old injury on their right leg that had probably been broken. To finish the lesson he looked up at the students and pointed out the young man who made the print. To our surprise the young man lifted up his trousers to reveal a deep scar on his right leg where he had had a compound fracture around 10 years earlier. All of this from looking at a set of prints for five minutes!

It is believed that, by carefully examining the track, gifted trackers look for over 2,000 things in one print, including direction travelled, pace, possible injuries (past and current), bodily functions (e.g. bladder full or empty), what the person or animal may have looked at while walking.

There are three things that a tracker observes that we can apply to help us ensure we are doing the things that we should be doing:

the direction we have been travelling;
the speed that we are travelling at; and
the mindset we have been using.

All of these are powerful methods we can use to increase our self-awareness and identify whether we have been staying on path or not.

Tracking the direction

Trackers identify the direction an animal is travelling by looking at the outside of the print. By studying the outside edges, a seasoned tracker can notice the shift in movement that will determine the next step and a series of prints can identify both the overall direction as well as the future direction to be travelled.

The prints may show an animal was travelling in a particular direction but moved to the left to avoid something or was distracted by something lurking to the left of the animal. In mapping our past activity, we can start to identify if our direction is still on course or if something has distracted us.

By mapping activities or steps we have actually taken, we can identify if we are using the best sequence or order. We may find that by changing the order of some activities or steps, we could have arrived at our destination more easily or sooner. These steps may have been a specific task we completed ourselves or the steps we took to interact with others.

No matter which was the case, both need to be objectively looked at to identify if the objective was accomplished and if the steps taken were the most effective. This allows us to ask ourselves are we getting our order right and is there a better approach than the one taken?

By identifying previous tasks and behaviour we can start to answer 'Is this the direction that I should be heading in?' and 'Am I taking the best steps possible based on what I want to achieve?'

Tracking the speed

Trackers can identify the pace or speed of an animal based on two factors. The distance between prints indicates the gait or speed – the farther apart the prints, the faster the animal was moving. More seasoned and expert trackers can determine speed by looking at the bottom, or floor, of the print.

In getting things done, we needs to look at the speed or pace of our own activity. We need to identify the steps we have taken – were they at a manageable pace with a conscious thought process or rapidly thrown together because they were the most obvious and there was no time to consider alternatives?

As previously mentioned many people are stuck in the Busyness Syndrome and turn everything into a speed game just to stay busy. This often results in poor decisions and activity that may take them off path, or which may need to be redone because the quality was poor. In tracking the speed, you need to identify the pace of your approach and decisions and examine if they were the most effective – or if there is a better approach that could be used next time.

Tracking the mindset

The most gifted trackers in the world can also identify the mindset of the animal they are tracking. They can identify tiny signs that show the animal is getting fatigued, is frightened or has gone into the 'hunting zone' as they stalk prey. For native people the tracks provided a window into the soul of the animal and this was one of the most revered and important signs to recognize. It provided the strong spiritual link to the animal and the environment that kept the people connected to the world around them.

By reflecting on our mindset while we were taking action, we get a much deeper understanding of what is driving us. It allows us not only to ask if we are on path, but also to ask the deeper question of why we are on this path. This can be a powerful approach allowing us to identify the true motivations beneath our actions. It can be quite confronting as it encourages us to strip away the excuses and clarify the real reason we are doing something.

In *Mindset: The new psychology of success*, Carol Dweck provides brilliant insight into the importance of mindset. Her research has found that the view that people adopt for themselves profoundly affects the way that they lead their life. She identified two distinct mindsets that determine whether people are successful in adapting to the world around them. The first is the Fixed Mindset: the belief that your traits are set for life. This includes the idea that people are born with a certain amount of intellect, personality and character that doesn't change. Dweck found these people felt the need to constantly prove their ability. The alternative is the Growth Mindset, based on the belief that your basic qualities are things you can cultivate through your efforts. This is all about learning from mistakes and using those insights to grow to the next level. Dweck's research shows that people who have a Growth Mindset are generally more fulfilled than those without because they can learn to fulfil their potential.

By examining your mindset you can start to identify what may be limiting your ability to complete the things that you want to achieve.

By tracking your past and current direction, speed and mindset, you increase your self-awareness and ensure that you are not operating on mental autopilot. More importantly, this method allows you to start reading the signs to determine if you are doing the right things in the right order based on recent activity.

Practical Exercise.

Write a list of the activities that you have been investing your time in over the past two to four weeks and estimate the amount of time you have spent in each of these areas.

If possible, group these activities under broad headings of a similar nature to help gain further perspective.

Next start looking at the speed or pace of your activity. Score yourself on a scale of 1–10 with 10 running at high speed and 1 barely moving. Ask yourself why you were moving at that speed? Did it help you or hinder you in getting the results you were after?

Finally, take a look at your mindset during this timeframe. What word or label would you put on it? Was it focused, distracted, frantic, scared, empowered? Once you have identified what your mindset was, ask if it served you? Was it the best frame of mind to facilitate doing the things you wanted to do in the order that you should have done them?

Strategy 2: Seek wisdom of elders

For many of us it can be difficult, on our own, to identify if we are on the right path. Sometimes we are so busy we do not have a perspective on what we are doing or how we are doing it. We often need to get someone else who can see us for who we truly are to provide an objective perspective that can assist us.

As we get older we gain more wisdom through life experiences either through trial and error or through observation over time. Unfortunately, Western society does not always regard older people as valuable or as a resource to be used to share knowledge. Many people make the mistake of looking to famous celebrities or sports stars for wisdom. They falsely believe that these people have wisdom, rather than just being physically gifted, or having the good fortune to appear on a reality television program that made them famous. They forget that many of the elders around them have more life experience and wisdom that can be a learning resource.

Native people had a deep respect for their elders. They viewed them as wise guides who held a vast array of knowledge that could be shared. Elders were sought out for wisdom and guidance when any major decision needed to be made. For Native American tribes, before a young warrior embarked on their Vision Quest to get the answers to their future, they would seek guidance from the wisdom of the tribal council of elders. In the Orient, a martial arts student would ask their teacher (Sensei in Japan, Shifu in China) for advice to guide them.

Elders also took a different approach in primitive times compared to today. Rather than sharing their knowledge by telling people exactly what to do they would find ways to share the wisdom so that it had strong meaning. This often came in the form of stories and parables using a Native American method commonly referred to as 'Coyote Teaching'.

This form of teaching requires the learner to fully embrace and understand what they are learning both on a mental and a physical level. The learner cannot just be told the answer and move on to the next item. They need to actively and consciously think about the answer at a deeper level.

To fully appreciate the difference, you only need to look at learning a new concept for the first time from a book as compared to experiencing it in life. I remember reading about how to make fire by creating a primitive bow drill. This technique uses a bow to move a wooden spindle back and forth on another piece of wood to generate friction, which leads to fire. Just reading about how to do it will never replace the first-hand experience.

Gripping the bow in one hand and pushing down to keep the wooden spindle in place on the other piece of wood is something primal that is hard to describe. As you increase the movement of the bow, it turns the spindle and you smell the burning of the wood. Reading about it on the internet can't provide the deep sense of fulfilment that comes when you generate enough friction to create an ember that you cradle in a nest of fibres and twigs and gently blow into to create fire. Even writing these words now brings back the deep sense of satisfaction that I felt when I first created my own fire by my own hands almost 25 years ago.

Since many native people did not have formal classrooms or text books, they used teaching methods that were practical.

Students see and experience what they are learning so it stays with them, rather than the typical short-term memorisation that occurs in many schools today. It is also great to see a number of teachers and schools challenging the norm and using Coyote Teaching in the classroom to bring concepts to life.

This short-term approach to learning is also happening on the internet and in the digital world. For most people quickly reading something on a screen will not get it into their medium- or long-term memory, so although the time was invested, the end benefit of attaining knowledge is lost. With people being able to remember less, many resort to external storage devices to remember things for them, which is leading to lazy minds and lazy thinking.

Council of Elders

To help stay on path, we should seek the council of elders. Their vast experience and insight can help provide us with a new perspective and allow us to re-evaluate what we are doing. How often have you had a conversation with an elder in your life with whom you had a special connection? This could be a grandparent or a favourite aunt or uncle you trusted because they held unconditional love for you. If you were fortunate enough, you may also remember a crucial conversation you had with them where they acted as a guide or signpost. They may have listened to you talk about your challenges and asked a few questions or shared a few stories from their own life that provided understanding and insight.

By seeking out elders we can ask them to share their wisdom with us based on our current circumstances. It can be very helpful to get thoughts, questions and concerns out in the open with someone who has experience and wisdom to draw on to assist us.

A true elder operates on a different level to the rest of society. They do not seem to get caught up with the hustle and bustle of the trivial things occupying everyone else's mind. This is what separates them from everyone else and gives them the unique ability to transcend the everyday world. They look at things from a much deeper perspective and have the ability to look at things over time.

The Three Keys: Wisdom, Mastery and Mentor

Who they are and what they can offer is what makes elders so valuable. Whether they come from a life of struggle or of privilege, whether they are famous or unknown, does not impact on the insights they can offer. Elders who can provide such guidance have acquired three key areas: their wisdom; an area of mastery; and the ability to mentor.

The first area of insight is the wisdom they have gained through experience. To me, wisdom is the ability to think, act and advise using knowledge, experience and understanding.

In seeking an elder, you are seeking their wisdom. You are asking for their advice based on their experience. A true elder does not spit out responses like Google. They do not randomly give shallow responses without deeper thought. They often use their wisdom to look beyond the question asked and use this to provide a much broader perspective. Those holding the power of wisdom often possess the ability to see the future potential beyond what currently exists. They can look into the future and see possible impacts that are often missed by short-sighted perspectives.

The second area of insight is mastery. Through their life experience they have developed a deep understanding of a specific skill. It could be cooking, painting, architecture or quilting or any of the ancient skills such as hunting, tracking or making baskets. The specific area of mastery is not the important factor, the process that they went through to become a master is. When someone achieves a level of mastery it provides them with a deeper appreciation of what it takes to accomplish this result.

In his book *Mastery*, best-selling author Robert Greene encapsulates what it takes to achieve mastery. He describes how someone who has mastered a particular skill has followed a particular journey in acquiring that skill. Through practice, they have mastered the basics and transcended them to make it appear easy and effortless. Greene studied great masters in history such as Leonardo da Vinci, Albert Einstein and Buckminster Fuller as well as modern-day masters such as neuroscientist V.S Ramachandran, Robotics Engineer Yoky Matsuoka and US Air Force fighter pilot ace Cesar Rodriguez. He found that mastery is not the result of genetics or privilege, but of effort and process and that mindset was important to achieve it.

When someone achieves mastery in a particular skill, they have evolved to a higher level of understanding. They have put in the time, energy, effort and focus required to provide them with a healthy dose of resilience and insight that others lack. This allows them to have a deeper appreciation and perspective of what someone may be going through when trying to learn a new skill or determine a new direction.

The ability to mentor is the third key quality of a true elder. The word 'mentor' comes from Greek mythology. When Odysseus went off to fight in the Trojan War, he left his trusted older friend, Mentor, in charge of both his sons and his estate. Mentor was not only to teach the boys to fight, he was also to instil in them a sense of right and wrong and provide them with the knowledge they would need to be successful in life.

Mentors, rather than speaking or randomly verbalising their thoughts, take a different approach, one that is built on trust and respect. An elder, in a mentoring role, often shows people alternatives by asking two distinct types of questions. The first set of questions is the 'what' questions that they ask to determine what it is that is actually being asked. This provides them not only with knowledge about the person asking the question, it also provides them with insights into how they perceive the world around them.

The second set of questions ask 'why'. Specifically they seek to clarify why the first question is being asked. It is used to uncover the real reason why someone is seeking advice or asking a specific question.

An elder provides wisdom, has mastery, and, as a mentor, can help people to stay on path. As a trusted advisor they can help a person gain perspective and move beyond their current mindset.

Translocate

The second method involves taking the time to gain perspective from an elder's point of view. It requires you to translocate away from any attachment to your current situation and ask the question, 'what would they do?'

This can also be a very useful approach as it is not dependent on another person. It does require a bit of personal role playing to help shift beyond the confines of one's own mind, however the benefits can be significant.

The way this works is that you take on the persona of an elder or someone that you respect. This can provide valuable insight based on their perspective. It involves asking yourself a series of questions to help shift beyond your current mindset. This is not new – people have done this throughout time. In fact, Peter Sander wrote *What Would Steve Jobs Do*? in which he encourages readers to view things from Steve's perspective and use this approach to help them think differently. Regardless of who the person is that you are using, it can be a helpful exercise.

To be most effective, one would still look at the situation from the three perspectives of an elder including wisdom, mastery and mentoring. For wisdom, you may ask what would this person say about the situation that I face. For mastery, you may ask what was something they mastered in their life that they might use to reflect on this situation. For mentoring, you may ask both what is the real question that is being asked as well as why is it important?

Practical Exercise.

As previously mentioned, it can be very helpful to translocate and ask what an elder would do in order to be able to tap into their insights. To do this include try asking yourself some of the following questions:

Who would you ask advice from?

Why would you ask them?

What wisdom would they give you? What would they see that you cannot? What perspective would they take if they were in your situation?

What is an area of mastery that they have achieved? How would they relate this area of mastery to your current situation? What advice might they share?

If they were to mentor you what would they do? If they were to ask you to summarise the question that you have into one sentence, could you do it? If so, what is it?

If they were to ask you why you have this question or why it is so important to you, what would you say?

Strategy #3: Listen to inner vision

In addition to tracking our past activity and seeking the wisdom of elders, one of the most powerful strategies we can use is based on our intuition and what native peoples called inner vision.

Inner vision is the voice that comes from deep within our soul. It is not the voice of the head that uses logic and facts to make decisions and justify actions. It is on a deeper level that is genetically linked into intuition, which has been with human beings since the dawn of time.

As well as intuition, inner vision is also described as premonition, hunch, gut feeling and sixth sense. There is scientific evidence that suggests that these premonitions are more than just the myth of psychics and fortune tellers. In a 2011 *Journal of Personality and Social Psychology* article by Daryl Bean from Cornell University, statistical evidence of the ability to anticipate a future event without any known physical or biological method was found and investigated. The study involved over 1,000 participants and revealed statistically significant results that supported the existence of this ability in eight out of nine experiments. In essence, the research supports the hypothesis that inner vision and intuition guide decisions and influence outcomes.

Think back to a time when you knew something deep inside to be true. It did not come from your head or your mind. It came from somewhere more connected with the core of who you are. You had no hard evidence, no statistical basis to influence you at the time, you just knew it was correct.

It could have been an inner voice that let you know that something was going to happen, or constant thoughts that kept coming into your consciousness about something you should do. It may have concerned something very simple or something larger and more important. Either way, that thought became reality – there is no such thing as coincidence.

Because of the distractions of the modern-day world, tuning into our inner vision can be a challenge. Taking the time to listen to what our intuition is telling us can be difficult with all the background noise and activity that fills our minds. However, there are ways to help us build this inner vision and tap into this valuable resource.

Concentric rings

Many native people looked for things occurring around them on multiple levels – in the physical, as well as the spirit or energy world. They would look at the relationship between the two to help them identify patterns and reasons for why things occurred.

Concentric Rings are the impacts of energy that they looked for. Based on their observation of the natural world they knew they were there, although they could not see them. When a stone is dropped into a calm pond of water, a ripple of concentric rings quickly expands and moves outward until they come into contact with something else. This effect can be seen both in nature and between people – rings of energy that one person constantly creates that can be sensed by others.

I was first taught about concentric rings when learning to hunt prey. When I asked the best way to stalk a deer on order to get close, I was told not to worry so much about the deer as the bird. I was a bit confused as I was not hunting a bird then. I was taught that the bird will see you moving and will give an alarm call that echoes through the woods. The alarm will be passed on by another bird that may be a couple of kilometres away. The end result of these concentric rings is the deer, which may be over 5km away, already knows you are in the woods.

Concentric rings are also found between people. If you walk into a room you can sometimes sense that two people have just had an argument, even though they don't say anything that suggests it. You have encountered this concentric ring. Although you did not witness the argument, you can sense the energy and as we say, 'You could cut the air with a knife.'

Concentric rings can be used to help us get in touch with the things we truly should be doing and the order in which we should be doing them – without getting distracted by other things.

Look, listen and feel

There are numerous ways to get in touch with your inner vision. You need to find a way that allows you to access your deeper levels. One of the simplest methods is to use the look, listen and feel approach.

Some people can 'see the way forward' when they visualise their thoughts. This may come in the form of a phrase or image that comes into their mind.

Others can look at the energy and concentric rings they are giving off. It may be looking at the passion or excitement of energy that 'lights you up' when you talk about it. It can also be what people notice when your energy deflates as you talk about what lies ahead.

Sometimes visualising what you and your energy look like can be useful. What do you see? What image are you projecting? How would others interpret your energy? Would they believe it or would they see that you are hiding something that you should really be doing or focusing on. These are all useful questions to consider.

Everyone hears voices in their head. This is the self-talk that we have that influences us. It can be both negative and positive, but it can also be a guide to assist us in making decisions and identifying the path ahead. Your inner vision can often be found in a voice that comes from deep within your soul. It is telling you a message you know you should listen to, even if it is difficult. We can often hear what our intuition is telling us to do, but we let the distraction of the mind get in the way.

When some of us get a deep feeling inside our soul we know our inner vision is speaking to us. It may not come in the form of pictures or words, but it comes to us through a deep-seated feeling of knowing. It is almost as if a wave of confidence pours over us and we have no doubt about the message that we have just received. For some, this can be a powerful insight that helps them to stay true to their path – as long as they pay attention to what they feel.

Modern-day Vision Quest

Ancient people from around the world participated in quests and listened to visions to help them stay true to their path. Native Americans in particular used a Vision Quest as a way to allow an individual to transform from their current reality and venture into a new environment that would encourage a new dimension in thinking and being.

They used ceremonies and rituals to prepare the young warrior for an experience that would shape their character and guide them for the rest of their life. The process often started with gathering insights from elders and a Sweat Lodge ceremony that was designed to 'cleanse the soul' and prepare them for their journey.

The young warrior would then walk out into the wilderness with no food, water or supplies until they received their visions or insights. The length of time varied depending on what the person experienced and could last for days or even weeks. It is thought that stress put on the human body quietens the mind and allows you to reconnect with your inner vision and sense what is truly important.

Many people today do not need to push themselves physically to have a break away from the norm. Modern-day Vision Quests are taken by people across the world to help them break with routine and get a fresh perspective. In academia, it is called a sabbatical, a period that gives teaching staff time to re-inspire their mindset and refresh their thinking.

In Aboriginal culture people go on walkabout. They often do not have a set agenda or a specific destination in mind, they just trust that the process of moving to new environments will bring higher levels of enlightenment and a stronger connection to what is important.

Some of the leading and most innovative minds in our modern world take Vision Quests to do the same. Bill Gates, the founder of Microsoft, is known to take retreats of up to seven days during which he completely unplugs from modern technological devices (no small feat for a person that made his billions in this field!). Rock star entrepreneur Richard Branson believes in these escapes so much that he purchased a couple of islands to provide a place for people to go and pursue introspection. He initially purchased Necker Island in the British Virgin Islands as an escape to recharge the batteries and Makepeace Island near Noosa as his escape in Australia.

Regardless of the approach one uses, the importance of checking in with one's inner vision is an important strategy that can be used to help keep you on path.

These three key strategies help to build awareness and make sure that you are on path. More importantly, they help to clarify that the right decision has been made. The strategies act like the needle on a compass – constantly indicating the direction you need to go. They also act as a guide to help you determine the important decisions that need to be made and the tasks that you should be focusing on.

Practical Exercise.

Here are some exercises to help you get in touch with your inner vision.

If you were to look at your concentric rings and your energy what would they be showing you? Fear? Confidence? On Autopilot?

If you were to picture images in your head of what questions you should be asking or what you should be considering, what images would you see?

What are the voices in your head telling you to do? More importantly what are the voices in your heart and your soul telling you to do?

What intuitions have you had in the past that you did not listen to but should have?

What are you feeling about the decision you need to make or the actions you have been taking? What should you be feelng if you are on track?

Chapter 3

Guidelines to Getting Your Order Right

Determining if what you are doing is the right thing is important and the three strategies I have given you provide guidelines to help you with this process. Also having the ability to clearly identify and prioritise the steps that need to be taken to accomplish more and their correct order is also important. Too often people make a decision about something and blindly act, without taking the time to identify the sequence of actions required to achieve what they desire.

Imagine that you are about to embark on a journey to a destination you have never travelled to before. You have an idea of where you want to go but you do not have the aid of modern-day technology, such as Google Maps.

How would you start? What would you do to ensure that you could plan your course from one location to the next? What method would you use to make sure that you stayed on path and did not get distracted by other things along the way? All of these are considerations that are helpful when identifying your strategy to advance.

Mapping your order: Five simple principles

There have been numerous books written on how to get things done. Many of the strategy and productivity books offering a range of solutions make things overly complex. They provide lots of steps you can take or they require an engineering degree to decipher the flow charts and decision models they propose.

For over 25 years I have worked with some of the largest and most successful companies to help them identify the way forward. The people mapping their strategies have often made things too complex for others to understand. I clearly remember assisting a large corporate organization in the early 2000s with their Strategic Plan. They gave me a copy of their previous 100 page Strategic Plan from five years earlier.

When I asked them why it was so large, the Head of Strategy said that they needed to put everything into one document to make it easier for people. I then asked the leadership team to think about their previous Strategic Plan and individually write down the top five business objectives and the three to five initiatives that supported each of these objectives. What happened? They could not do it.

The Strategic Plan they had created was so complex and all-encompassing they could not recall what it was. The person who typed up the document could recall what it entailed, but in a company with over 1,000 staff the limitations of what they had created was obvious. It is not surprising that when we asked them what was in the document, they came up short – it was not simple enough for people to remember, relate to or act on.

What if there were a simple process, one that people throughout the ages have instinctively turned to help them stay on track and one that was flexible enough to take the mindset of the modern world into account?

In working with organizations around the world, I have found that there are ways to simplify strategic plans. I often notice five recurring basic steps to map the sequence that can be used to stay on track, that can help both individuals or groups of people get their order right. These principles, although very simple, allow you to see the way forward and assist in fast-tracking progress towards success. They provide a framework that allows for flexibility and exploration.

Many individuals and companies try to make their overall plan too detailed and never give themselves the opportunity to map a framework for progress that is more efficient. I do not recommend the common over-planning that occurs in the corporate world, but I do recommend a process that can simply and easily identify a method that can be modified to increase the opportunity for success.

Principle 1: Identify the objective in a simple way
Principle 2: Visually explore options
Principle 3: Select the order with care
Principle 4: Capture what not to do
Principle 5: Take action and make time in time

The best way to follow these principles is to imagine you are on a journey to a faraway place you have never been to. You can use this approach to help you get things done and map the order.

The aim is to not create a massive strategic plan, but to use these principles to quickly and easily identify the way to progress. Depending on the importance of what you are planning, you can invest more time using some of the more traditional methods of planning by adding additional layers of strategies, tactics and milestones.

Principle 1: Identify the objective in a simple way

The first step is one of the most important. It requires you to identify the decision you have to make or the result that you are hoping to achieve. It cannot just be a random thought floating around in your head, but something you can clarify and write down in one sentence.

To do this you need to know what it is that you are trying to do. It has to be simple and not overly complex. The simpler it is, the easier it is to remember and you are more likely to identify a good order or strategy for achieving it.

Some good examples of simple objectives include:

- Delegate tasks to staff.
- Write a book.
- Spend more time with my family.

These are good examples because they are simple and clear. They do not need to have timeframes, analytical details or specific measurements linked to them – that comes at a later stage. This is about getting what you want to accomplish clear and using this as a way to get your order of activity right.

Some poor examples include:

- Increase internet marketing sales penetration by 15% by first quarter 2016 with a conversion ratio of 25%.
- Have a 60,000-word book with a leading publisher by 1 January 2016.
- Exercise five times per week for 90 minutes keeping heart rate at 75% of maximum

While these examples are interesting, they are complex and trying to identify this level of detail at this stage can be counterproductive. Finding simple objectives can be difficult given the brainwashing the corporate world has put around measurable goals using the S.M.A.R.T. (Specific, Measurable, Achievable, Relevant, Time-related) method. While this approach can be useful, it is distracting at the beginning because it makes you forget what you are trying to accomplish. Our aim is to capture a simple goal and not try to put all of the variables into one sentence.

From thought to reality

There is also something very important when you take this idea or end result and commit it to paper. Writing it down has the potential to transform a random thought into a clear objective.

I have worked with many people who have started taking action in one direction without having clarified what it is they are trying to achieve. The result is often a lot of wasted time and energy in activities that did not support their true direction. Not only can this lead to exhaustion, it can also lead to thousands of hours and dollars being invested in areas that have no relevance. Remember, by following your own Sacred Order you are making it easier and clearer to achieve the result you are after.

Capture the why

Another useful approach to identify what it is that you want to achieve is to capture why you want to achieve it. Identifying the true reason why you want this result can provide the important reminder that you may need when you are taking action toward your goals. It can also be used to create a saying or a slogan to be used to help guide future decisions.

Leading up to the 2000 Sydney Olympics, the Great Britain Rowing Team needed inspiration. After years of struggling to determine the necessary ingredients to win an Olympic medal, they realised they were making things too complex by considering everything they needed to include in their training, their boat, their equipment and their racing strategy. They came up with the simple mantra: 'Does it make the boat go faster?' They based all decisions on this and if it did not answer this question they disregarded it. After they won the Gold Medal at the Sydney Olympics, rower Ben Hunt-Davis wrote his book *Will It Make the Boat Go Faster?* and shared the knowledge of how they used this approach to win.

Writing down a simple and clear goal crystallises the objective in your mind. This makes it easier for you to start getting your order right and ensure the steps to fall into place.

Principle 2: Visually explore options

Once you have identified specifically what it is that you want to accomplish, deciding on options that can be taken is important. For many of us this is a fairly natural problem-solving process that we were taught in school. Common sense would say that it should be easy to identify four to six steps to take to achieve anything, but this raises the question of why so many of us stick to the same routine and the same line of thinking? We often hear of brilliant minds that identify new ways of doing things that inspire us, and wonder how they do it.

In common planning terminology, when you ask what needs to be done and how you should you do it, you generally look at possible strategies and the specific tactics of those strategies. I often find that, when people try to identify every specific detail, they get bogged down with data and soon stop the progress of mapping their overall strategy.

When we try to identify options we can take toward goals, we naturally consider the ideas or thoughts inside our head. Who hasn't struggled with trying to easily identify a number of steps to take? It can be challenging to clarify because of all the other thoughts that are flying through our mind. This can confuse us further as numerous ideas and thoughts start running together.

Visual, auditory and kinaesthetic methods

Research shows that people have different learning and thinking strategies. Some early researchers challenged traditional methods of teaching based on their observations of how some people can reach higher levels of understanding.

In his 1983 book *Frames of Mind: The theory of multiple intelligences*, Harvard Professor Howard Gardner identified visual–spatial learning as one of the eight multiple intelligences that we have. He challenged the popular notion that logical linear thinking and high intelligence (or IQ) was required for success.

Another group of researchers, Walter Barbe, Raymond Swassing and Michael Milone, also challenged traditional teaching methods in their 1979 book *Teaching Through Modality Strengths: Concepts and practices.* This is considered the precursor to what is now commonly referred to as the VAK (Visual, Auditory, Kinaesthetic) method of learning or understanding i.e. we learn and organize thoughts according to three methods.

The first is through the Visualising style. Simply put, this involves the use of pictures, shapes, diagrams, images and colours to help increase understanding and retention. The second is the Auditory style, which uses listening, tone and rhythm and the third method is Kinaesthetic i.e. body movement, tactile or touching experiences and gestures to increase understanding.

While using all three styles is the best way to increase an individual's learning and comprehension, it is believed that the largest percentage of the population have a bias towards learning and understanding using a visual approach.

This is why I recommend mapping ideas and options onto paper or a whiteboard to help you visualise what they are.

There are numerous techniques you can use to capture these thoughts. Some people randomly write down what comes to mind on a sheet of paper allowing them to identify steps they need to take. Others prefer to use a whiteboard where they can put up their thoughts and move them around as they come rushing out from the brain.

Tony Buzan is the inventor of a technique called Mind Mapping and an expert on the brain and memory. He is a best-selling author and has written over 100 books including: *Use Your head: Innovative learning and thinking, The Power of Creative Intelligence* and *How to Mind Map*. His techniques are believed to be similar to those Leonardo da Vinci and others used to take their thinking to a higher level.

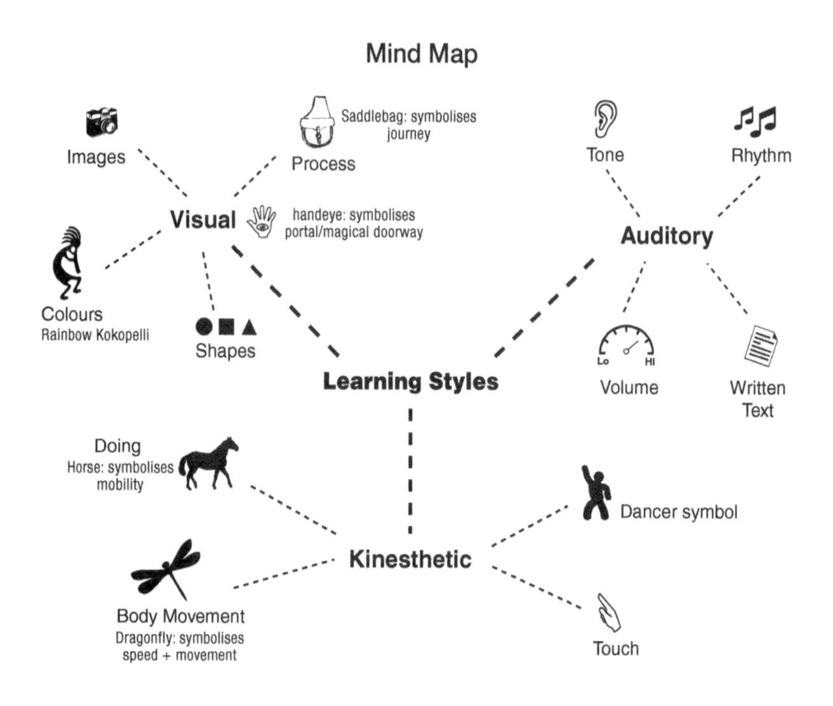

Mind Mapping is a technique that can be used to capture the thoughts in your mind and transfer them onto paper so the information can be easily seen. This allows you to start to identify patterns and hierarchies that can be used to help organize your thoughts. Buzan also believes that these Mind Maps have a number of things in common, including a structure that starts in the centre and radiates outward with the use of colour, symbols, lines and images that make it easier to identify, understand and organize. He also believes that this process more accurately mirrors how the brain shifts from one idea to the next.

His books really are worth a read as they provide a much deeper understanding of how to mind map, which does help to organize thoughts in a clear and simple way.

Of course you do not have to follow any particular methodology to identify the steps that you need to take, the important thing is to get these ideas out of your head and onto paper so you can see what they are.

Principle 3: Select the order with care

One of the best approaches to take in plotting your course is to select the order or sequence of action with care. This is often overlooked as people randomly take action on the steps they have identified and forget the importance of a sequence and how this can impact other people and the desired end result.

It is useful to ask the question: 'What needs to be done first and how does this make it easier to take the next step?' You may also notice patterns or levels of significance that will help you weigh up which step to take and in which order.

You may need to gather additional information to fully understand what goes into accomplishing the tasks you have mapped. This is especially true if the actions identified require other people to be informed, involved or empowered to act. Too many strategic plans have been derailed when managers have simply told subordinates what to do.

In working with leadership teams to identify their way forward, I often use a concept called Ranking Order. Once the group has determined what actions to take, they use a ranking system to identify what step comes next. The individual steps are written on index cards which are pinned onto large storyboards. It is easy to see what needs to be prioritised and the cards can be moved around.

A brief discussion helps to understand the possible tactics that support each step. The group votes on which step needs to be completed first. This is followed by the next step and so on until each of the actions has been assigned a numerical Rank Order. Although this sounds extremely simple, by using this visual process, I have been able to help groups of corporate executives agree on a way forward in 60 minutes. They have already spent one or two days on their own debating and arguing, because they did not have a methodology that was clear and easy to identify.

You can often get caught up in trying to determine which step must come before another when there may be no advantage to this. If this is the case, do not waste time trying to justify why one step needs to be done first, place them in order and move on to the other areas that need to be prioritised.

Mapping out the order is one of the most significant processes that are often overlooked. Short-sighted managers will say the results justify the means. If, to get the job done, they had to belittle, yell and intimidate their people, then they believe they were successful.

The challenge with this linear line of thinking is what happens next? What happens when staff start to resent the manager and look for ways to balance the relationship? What happens to their productivity, innovation and motivation? What occurs to the energy they share with their colleagues and the flow-on to customers after they have been treated this way? Taking care to ensure the order is right will result in better relationships, better outcomes and a better workplace.

Principle 4: Capture what not to do

One useful strategy to stay focused on what you have committed to, is to identify what distractions may take you off path. Too many times someone identifies a strategy they want to take and gets sidetracked by something else that is not part of their plan and does not contribute to what they want to accomplish.

Once a commitment is made, it is important to identify the other options that will be sacrificed. Creating a list of alternative options that will not be pursued can be as important as the steps identified and committed to. With all of the distractions that occur in today's fast-paced world, using a strategy to limit these interferences is important. This is as relevant today as it has been for hundreds of years.

Burn the ship

Hernan Cortez was one of the first Spanish explorers looking for riches and opportunities in the new world in the 1500s. He was made famous when he burned the boats that forced his soldiers to fight and eventually conquer the Aztecs in what is now Mexico. Now that really is sacrificing a distraction that could have got in the way of his objective!

While I do not recommend burning things to the ground, the commitment that he demonstrated is now legendary. For people to break a habit, they often need to sacrifice the things that pushed them into the habit. In his book *The Power of Habit: Why we do what we do and how to change*, Charles Duhigg refers to a 2006 Duke University researcher who found that more than 40% of the actions people performed each day weren't actual decisions, but habits. This is why it is so important for people to identify what they should not be doing to consciously capture the habits that they normally would use in the past.

If you are prone to distractions, it can be useful to ask 'What am I willing or have to sacrifice to reach the objectives that I have?' By identifying these distractions that may take you off track you focus your approach to allow you to achieve your goals.

Identifying the things that will take you off track before you get started, this allows you to increase your chance of success and can save you valuable time.

Principle 5: Take action and make time in time

It is surprising how some people can get an amazing amount of things done in the same timeframe other people cannot get anything done. We all have the same amount of time and we cannot control time, but we can control the way we use our time.

An important principal to remember when taking action towards a goal is to continue the momentum. Keeping focused on the end goal and the 'why' is an important strategy that you can use to stay focused.

Another important approach that I use is to fold time or make time in time. This is getting into a state of flow so that things start to feel effortless and you get smarter with the time you have available. It is a mindset and a state of mind that enhances senses and streamlines activity, whether it is mental or physical.

It can involve something as simple as taking time on a flight or taxi ride to plan and map out the next day's activities. Travel time is generally considered lost time because it is not a normal work environment and most people switch off (and watch the inflight movie or read a magazine). By harnessing this time you can significantly increase your output and gain time to focus on other priorities.

David Allen is a productivity expert who provides a number of be strategies that people can use to be more effective with their time. In his book *How to Get Things Done: The art of stress-free productivity* he views the biggest challenge to completing things is how people manage their activity with the time they have available. By not keeping focused on priorities and making conscious choices, Allen believes that the real issue that inhibits people's effectiveness is how they manage their actions.

Allen provides a range of strategies that can be used to help you stay active and productive. He has also developed an entire methodology around GTD (Getting Things Done) that focuses around increasing productivity.

Another approach is one advocated by *New York Times* Best Selling authors Jason Fried and David Heinemeier Hansson in their book *Rework*. They have captured the wisdom that they have learnt in founding their productivity software company, 37signals, which is now used by millions of people around the world. They actively discourage the use of formal business plans and how to focus on activity to create what you want.

Although written in the context of starting a business, they provide brilliant insights that can be used across organizations including the importance of starting, how a limited resources mindset (and reality) can increase innovation and how good enough is better than not starting at all. I find their book a series of inspirational messages that can help anyone to quickly and easily increase their activity in ways that challenge the normal lines of business thinking.

To get things done you need to focus on activity and continue focusing on doing the activity. This can be challenging given all the distractions that we have in the world today as previously mentioned. There are a couple of other techniques that can also make the activity that you need to do easier, turn them into a Project or a Game.

Make it a project

For some people the thought of having a number of tasks or actions to take does not motivate them, they need something more. It can be useful to turn an action into a project. A project is task that needs to be completed in a specific timeframe. It can be useful to have timeframes that are smaller and easier for us to see the progress that we have made in completing projects. A useful timeframe for a project can be one week, one month or even 90 days.

In *The New Rules of Management: How to revolutionise productivity, innovation and engagement by implementing projects that matter*, author and implementation guru Peter Cook shows how turning tasks into projects can make a massive difference in getting things done. The new rules of management require what Cook calls a 'relentless focus on implementation – which is the creation and execution of projects.'

To enable people to implement projects that matter, Cook has developed a Primary Implementation Model that includes Projects, Framework, Support and Accountability as the strategy to getting things done. By having strategies developed in each of these areas you can increase success. His book is definitely worth a read to anyone who wants to implement and get things done.

Make it a game

Everyone has played games before. We play sports games, card games, board games and computer games. Games have been a part of human life forever. They can be fun and rewarding. We have a different mindset when we play a game. We are motivated, focused and participating – all helpful traits for getting things done!

Dr Jason Fox is an expert on games. He has studied the essential ingredients of what makes a game fun and how these principles can be used to turn everyday work activity into something more. In his book *The Game Changer: How to use the science of motivation with the power of game design to shift behavior, shape culture and make clever happen* he shows how games are the same as any other activity – and can be used to get things done.

Games are simply the interplay of goals, rules and feedback. A good game is a goal-driven, challenge-intense and feedback-rich experience geared toward making progress. All games whether they are puzzles, sports games, strategy games, role play games, simulation games, training games or video games share the same essential three ingredients: goals, rules and feedback.

But here's the thing: nearly every other element of life shares those same three components. So nearly everything in life is a game. Any project is a game. There are goals (complete this project to bring the prototype into the next phase of implementation), rules (do it in less than six weeks and with less than $30,000), and feedback.

By turning tasks into a game you can shift your mindset and rewire your motivation to getting things done.

Regardless of how you take action and be productive, it is one of the keys to reaching your objectives. As the saying goes, the journey is just as important as reaching the destination. The way that you go about staying on your critical path and the order you take will determine if you do the right things, at the right time, in the right way.

Section 3

Business Critical Pathways

How does a leader in business get their order right? How do they do the things they know they should be doing rather than getting sidetracked by the pressures of business and the everyday world?

If we had more managers and employees listening to their inner vision, using the wisdom of elders and tracking their signs, we would live in a more enriched and fulfilled world. If we had more people staying focused on how to do things, rather than randomly reacting to stress, we would have an engaged workforce. When people go to work because they want to – rather than because they have to – organizations will more easily achieve sustainable results.

For the past 25 years across the United States, Europe, Asia and Australia I have had the opportunity to work with some truly incredible organizations where they did things in a way that showed they were getting their order right and staying on their critical path. These leaders and their employees seem to march to a different drum than many traditional companies.

The Sacred Order at Work

There are a number of key ingredients that organizations need to have to maximize their potential and accelerate down their critical path. There is also a hierarchy or 'Sacred Order' that many of the most successful businesses follow to ensure that they focus on the right things, at the right time, in the right way.

My close friend and author of eight books, Michael Henderson, captured what it is that these businesses have that others do not. For many decades as an anthropologist he studied tribes and what it was that allowed them to be adaptable and last through time. He noticed that these characteristics are also what many leading organizations have that separates them from the rest. They have three key ingredients they use to stay true to their critical path: cultures worth belonging to; leaders worth following; and work worth doing.

As many businesses also have customers, there is a fourth ingredient that is important, namely the customers that are necessary for the business to continue. Significantly, the organizations and businesses that seem to be getting this right are the ones that focus on customers worth having.

Sacred Order at Work

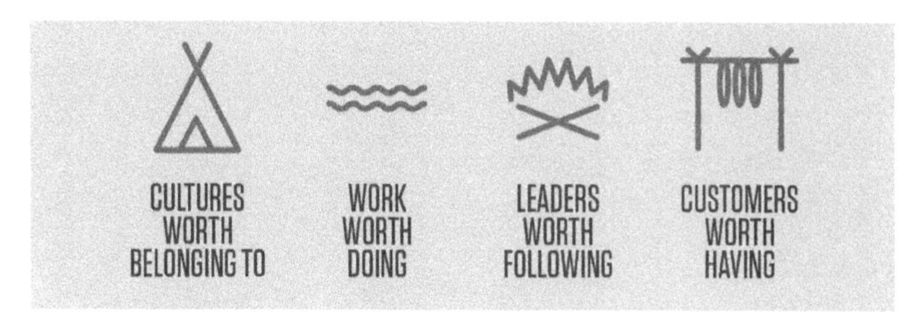

As in the Sacred Order of Survival, organizations need to ensure that they get their priorities right. This creates a hierarchy that can be identified and developed to ensure that their true potential can be reached. The challenge is that many organizations are mixing up their order. Rather than focusing on creating a positive culture or work environment for staff, they overfocus on customers. All their internal metrics and KPIs are about customers and customer satisfaction, and they neglect the other core ingredients necessary to create and maintain this customer focus.

If an employee does not work within a positive culture with leaders who motivate, inspire and challenge, and if they are constantly berated, belittled and made to feel dispensable, then it is more difficult for them to focus on the customer. By getting these priorities in the right order and the right time, you can leverage more sustainable performance.

Chapter 1

Cultures Worth Belonging to

This involves creating a place that provides people with a stronger sense of belonging than just work. A traditional company with a traditional structure will have their vision and value statement hanging on the walls in the boardroom. This, however, does not always mean that the ethos of this vision exists. In fact, in many of the companies that I have been called in to assist, the words on the wall have lost their meaning.

Have you ever worked for an organization that you were completely and 100% devoted to? Or do you know of someone that is so excited about the company they work for that they actively live and breathe it? They have a sense of pride and commitment that runs so deep they could not imagine working anyplace else. When you ask them what it is that the company does they often describe the way people are treated and the way things are done. They feel challenged, stretched, appreciated and fulfilled at the same time. This is when a culture worth belonging to has been created.

Businesses spend millions of dollars every year trying to identify the crucial elements of their culture. They invest in surveys in a desperate attempt to try to measure those elements. Culture can be a very complex thing and it can also be the crucial thing that separates a mediocre company from a great company. It is the special 'something' that puts a spring in employees' steps and takes performance to the next level.

Jim Collins is the international best-selling author of *Good to Great: Why some companies make the leap … and others don't*, which looks at what it is that companies do to become great. He looked at companies over a 15-year timeframe to ensure that the company was not a 'one hit wonder'. He also uses financial success, including profit and increase in stock value, to point out the tangible benefits of these activities. It is a must read for any business leader who wants to turn good results into great results. In his follow-up book with Jerry Porras, *Built to Last: Successful habits of visionary companies*, he took a more in-depth look at what companies do to turn great results into an great company that endures. What they found was that a visionary company has fundamental beliefs that let the staff know who they are and what they stand for. He also found that many of these companies create a cult-like following among their staff because they are such strong advocates.

Creating a culture worth belonging to is also at the top of the hierarchy. This means that if this is not created first, it is challenging, and it then takes longer to get the performance that many leaders are looking for. If this environment is not there, it is hard to get staff to feel motivated or be fulfilled in the work that they are doing. If you work in a toxic environment where you are always looking over your shoulder because you do not know which staff member (or manager) will be attacking you next, it is hard to have a positive approach with customers. .

When the culture of an organization is toxic, people automatically get on the defensive. Often this leads to them pursuing trivial activity in order to justify their position. It can also lead to people consciously slowing their productivity because they fear if they are too efficient the organization will want to 'downsize' them out of a job in the search for reduced expenses and increased profits. There is also a large body of research that shows when employees feel that their company does not appreciate or take care of them, then they want to even the score. This often results in these disenfranchised staff looking for ways to take things back. This activity can be as drastic as stealing things from the company they work for or taking excessive sick or stress leave to steal time from the company.

Organizations that have created a positive culture that people want to be a part of are the ones that attract (and retain) the best talent and are seen within their industry as a great place to work. In addition they are often viewed as the Thought Leaders in their industry because they have been able to harness the collective genius and talent of their people, which has allowed them to achieve higher results compared to their peers.

So, if you are leading a company, have you created a culture worth belonging to?

Do the energy and concentric rings that are found across departments foster a sense of pride and commitment in every employee to go the extra mile if required?

If not, you may need to ask what is missing and, more importantly, what needs to happen to get the culture right. What is your Sacred Order to get the culture where it needs to be?

Chapter 2

Leaders Worth Following

Many researchers believe the culture of an organization is established by its leaders. As an executive of a company they do have legal authority for what happens, but it is more than that. To be a leader worth following they have to fully embody the culture they are trying to create. They need to be a constant reminder and role model for the way things need to be done.

In the past an employee would blindly follow the leaders or managers of a company just because of their title. When someone was a CEO or Director of a Division there was instant authority and rigid organizational structures to keep communication constrained by these specific areas of power. The traditional pyramid top-down hierarchy in a company mandated that people communicate directly to their supervisor when they needed some new information or resources. It was considered political suicide to go outside the 'chain of command' and try to communicate or work with other departments.

Internal computer servers and email quickly tore down these traditional lines of communication and the hierarchal power they embodied. In the early days of this technology, it was not uncommon for an employee not familiar with the email system to accidently copy in the entire staff list. This mistake could not be taken back and there were plenty of embarrassing conversations that occurred when private communications were accidently broadcast across the entire company.

In the past management's power lay in the information they kept tightly controlled. Nowadays everyone can access information from numerous sources and quickly and easily share it with others.

This change has resulted in the traditional authority of people in management positions being questioned. Traditional managers no longer have the same positional power. In fact, many of the younger generation look at a person in management and ask the question (in their head or directly): 'What are you going to do for me as my manager? What can you offer me to keep me motivated and excited to be here?'

They have the belief that managers should earn their title through the demonstration of their skills and capabilities – and the ability to teach and mentor staff to do the same. The traditional corporate ladder where the next person in line for a manager's job was the one with the most years of seniority is now not accepted as an effective way to do business.

I remember working with a sales manager who was complaining about his younger sales consultants. 'They just don't want to follow instructions. When I was in their position, when my manager asked me to do something I did not question him, I just did it.'

He was living in the past when a person's job title demanded blind respect. What he missed is that his sales staff wanted to know *why* they were doing what he wanted them to do. They wanted to understand the reasoning behind it and have a chance to be involved and actively contribute to the thinking, rather than following orders in a robotic manner. They became demotivated when he did not provide this.

His sales staff had lost all respect for their manager because what they experienced from him was a series of orders barked at them. The environment they walked into every morning put them face to face with a dictator who treated them as if they were dispensable. They did not feel informed, included or valued by him. No wonder his staff turnover was almost 70% and he could not keep a sales consultant for longer than four weeks. The unfortunate thing was that he was blaming all of the sales performance issues on his 'younger staff' rather than recognizing that he was the problem. He was not a leader worth following and his sales staff let him know this by leaving.

The founder of Thought Leaders Global, leadership expert Matt Church, is a prolific author (not to mention a close friend and business partner). He is one of the most incredible minds I have come across and has his finger on the pulse of leadership. In his book *Amplifiers: The power of motivational leadership to inspire and influence* he identifies leaders worth following as amplifiers.

Amplifiers are the rare and extraordinary leaders who amplify the best in themselves and others. They amplify the messages that matter, amplify the positive mood in a culture and amplify the results achieved. They are masters of maximising human potential and developing other great leaders.

Think of a leader you know that you would follow. What is it that they do that would get you to follow them?

If you are a leader, what are you doing to get people to want to follow you? What daily activities or approach do you consistently demonstrate with your staff that turns them on and lights them up?

Do you have the wisdom of elders that we explored earlier? Do they seek you out for insights and for your mastery? If not, what do you need to do to earn this right?

Chapter 3

Work Worth Doing

Going to work and accomplishing something is vital to our human psyche. When we believe we are doing something bigger than ourselves, we gain a deep sense of fulfilment. Whether this is producing something tangible such as a product, delivering a service or seeing our ideas being put into use by others, we know that we have contributed.

Abraham Maslow developed his hierarchy of needs, which is widely used to describe the levels of motivation we have as human beings. Maslow's model is built on the belief that we gain our motivation from these needs. In other words, people's unconscious behaviour is driven by these areas that need to be fulfilled.

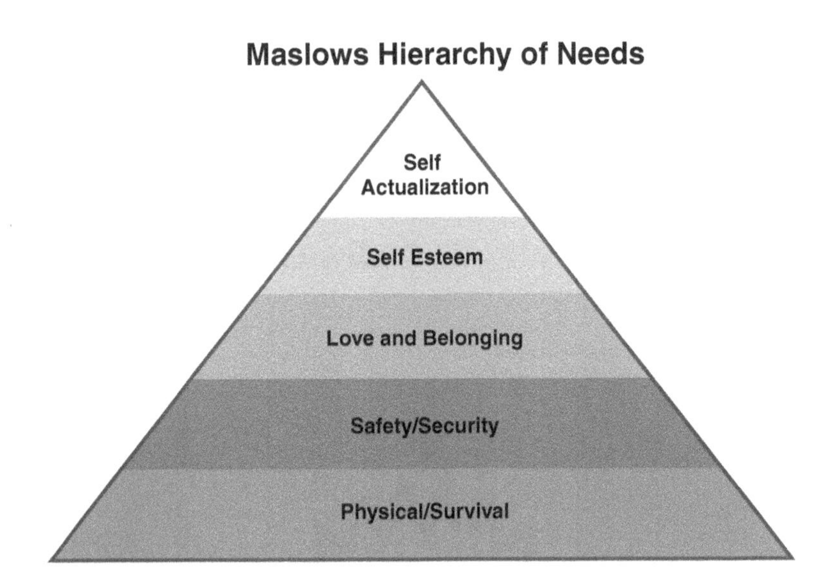

Physical needs

The hierarchy starts with our most basic need – physical survival. To fulfil this we need food, water, air, clothing and shelter from the environment. These instinctive survival needs unconsciously kick in when we feel under threat. Today, for most of us in the Western world, these basic needs are easily satisfied.

Safety needs

Once the immediate need to survive is taken care of, the next level is about safety or security for the longer term. Maslow identified four categories within this level including: personal security, financial security, health and wellbeing and security from accidents/illness. Physical security and the protection of our loved ones is knowing that you will not have to stay in a 'fight or flight' mindset at all times. It is knowing that you will be able to relax and not be afraid of others harming you.

Economic security includes employment and job security as well as the ability to earn an income. A certain peace of mind comes when you know you will be able to put food on the table for yourself and your family.

Health and wellbeing and safety against illness/accidents are also essential. It is human nature to want to be healthy and avoid getting sick. Just remembering when you were sick and had to spend a few days in bed with the flu can act as a natural deterrent to repeating the experience.

Protection from being taken advantage of by others is also integral to this safety need. This can include the need to protect yourself from being sued or taken advantage of by someone in a financial way. Think of the letters that people used to receive from 'a Nigerian prince' who wanted to give their family fortune to you as an unknown, deserving person. All you needed to do was transfer some money into their account so they would have your bank details. This method of financial deception has now gone online and some people are still being taken advantage of.

The need for love and belonging

This third level is the human need to be loved by others, getting the sense of belonging and connection from people around you – your immediate and extended family, work colleagues, the community and social groups. We all have this basic need to some extent – some people need constant companionship to feel complete, while others only need it in small doses.

I see this all the time when I present at large company conferences. Often the conference attendees only know a few people from their department. During the lunch break and between sessions they often congregate together, even though they regularly spend eight hours a day with each other at work. They have a connection with these people that provides them with a sense of belonging in the large mass of people around them.

The need for esteem

The fourth level is the need for self-respect and self-esteem. Esteem can be gained from others when we get attention and recognition in a way that shows we are valued. Self-respect comes from having a sense of self-confidence, independence and freedom to make decisions and choices. Unfortunately, research is starting to show that when this need is not fulfilled, there can be an increase in mental illness. As previously mentioned, I also believe this is why there is an increase in fear and anxiety in our society. People are not getting enough of this need fulfilled at the workplace and many, unfortunately, do not get it at home because other family members are so busy – so caught up in their own life.

The need for self-actualization

This highest level need is a person's ability to reach their full potential, whatever that may involve. It is about having goals and dreams and the ability to accomplish these in order to become the best we can be. It is about self-fulfilment and is also believed to include transcending self and pursuing higher goals that are more altruistic in nature.

As in the Sacred Order of survival for native people, Maslow believes that these needs follow a particular order or hierarchy. The highest need, Self-Actualization, cannot be reached until the previous needs are satisfied. This makes sense because, if your life is being physically threatened, the need for world peace will probably not be a priority.

When people do not have their needs fulfilled at work, they become disillusioned. Having work worth doing is difficult if the basic needs are not met. Another shift that has occurred over time in the workplace is that the nature and type of work has changed from the merely physical and tangible to the intangible. This means that more people have less opportunity or capability to gain self-respect and esteem.

As our society has developed to provide for the most basic needs, the higher level needs have become more of a conscious goal or, for some, an expectation. In the past, work provided this sense of accomplishment for most people. However, the nature of work and how we get these needs met is changing and we are now at a turning point.

Chapter 4

Customers Worth Having

Without customers, most businesses would not exist. They are an important part of any business and come in all shapes and sizes depending on the organization and the product or offering they promote. There are also different categories of customers depending on the degree of interaction and contact that they have with the organization.

Customer Categories

One-off Customers
Regular Customers
Loyal Customers
Advocate Customers

At the simplest level, there are four distinct categories that can be easily identified.

One-off Customers

The first level is that of One-off Customers. These are the customers who have very little interaction with or purchase little from a business. Often these are the one-off buyers who conduct only one transaction for products or services. They do not normally become regular customers. Either they were not impressed with the experience, or the item that they purchased is not something that is an ongoing need. A lot of businesses have many such customers who never return.

Regular Customers

These are customers that have purchased more than once from a business. They have an ongoing need that encourages them to continue to complete transactions for a product or service from the same business. Such customers are often not committed to any one brand, organization or product. They will continue to complete short-term transactions until they find another opportunity to purchase elsewhere (including at a reduced price or increased value offering).

Loyal Customers

This category of customers demonstrate their loyalty to a particular organization or business by returning for ongoing transactions over time. They are not actively seeking to find these products or services elsewhere because they are satisfied with the experience and service they have received. They will continue to return for a number of reasons including: convenience of location; familiarity; relationships with particular staff; and product quality. For many organizations these customers provide the majority of their business. Looking at a range of companies across a number of industries it is not uncommon to find that most of their ongoing sales are from these loyal customers. *Forbes Magazine* found that the Pareto Principle is alive and well across most businesses with 80% of their sales coming from 20% of their customers – the majority of them being the loyal ones. There are additional insights into this phenomenon in Perry Marshall's book *80/20 Sales and Marketing: The definitive guide to working less and making more.* Based on wider investigation, Marshall has drawn a further conclusion. Often the top 20% of customers also fall into a further 80/20 dynamic. In essence this means that the top 20% of the top 20% of customers can represent up to 60% of a business's overall sales.

Advocate Customers

These customers are more than loyal. They go out of their way to actively promote and encourage others toward a particular business. When friends or co-workers ask them to recommend a particular business, they promote the business and 'sell' the value that this business has provided for them. These are the customers that are sought after by organizations and businesses around the world. These committed customers generate millions of dollars in word-of-mouth advertising and generate additional customers. These are the most highly desired customers as they not only continue to return time after time because of their loyalty, they also bring in new customers.

Customer categories enable an organization to target customers. Many businesses fail to focus on the customers that are worth having. Rather than tracking and classifying customers, many organizations do not use customer data to develop a plan to increase their relationship and opportunities with these customers. By targeting customers worth having, a business can increase their opportunities, as well as stay in front of their competition.

How do you currently classify your customers? Are you focusing on the customers that matter the most to your business and what are you doing to let them know that they are important to you? If your staff were to be interviewed would they say that your Order is correct or that it is mixed up – focusing on customers without creating a culture that is supportive or having systems in place that make it easier to do so?

Unfortunately, time and time again I have been brought in to work with companies that have mixed up this order. They focus on the wrong areas before they have developed the foundation for success. Too often they put all their attention on customers before they have developed an internal culture worth belonging to and created an environment that encourages innovation, growth and honesty. This often results in a short-term fix that leads to a long-term issue.

When staff are not treated well, they do not stay, or if they do, their resentment can often be taken out on customers. Without a sense of connection and a positive culture that encourages individual accountability, people play the 'blame game' and pass responsibility to others or hide behind policy rather than going the extra mile.

By ensuring that your get your Sacred Order correct in business, you can increase your opportunity for success, inspire your people and create customer advocates. Once you achieve this success, there is continuing need to ensure that your organization, leaders and people remain on their critical path. Given the rapid changes in the way work is carried out and the disruptions impacting people, this is an ongoing imperative.

Chapter 5

How Work Has Changed

The nature of work has significantly changed over the past 300 years. Many of us don't appreciate the progress that has been made in a comparatively short time for civilisation to develop from the uncertain struggle for basic survival to comfortable living for the majority of people on the planet.

Back in the 1700s, unless you were born into royalty or privilege, life was hard. Many people struggled to feed themselves and their families. For the most part they were jacks-of-all-trades and used their wits and physical efforts to carve out a living – with no security over where the next meal would come from.

People had to make everyday things for themselves; family and friends helped to build their homes; they would spin their own thread and make their own clothing; and they would hunt, plant and harvest their own food. Most worked on the land, either on their own farms or as sharecroppers working someone else's land and making a meagre living from their efforts. Physical labour was the primary method of making a living. Education was not formalized and was limited – including reading and writing. It was not uncommon for children as young as eight to start working in the fields or around the home to contribute to the family's existence.

The Industrial Revolution ensured that the masses had a job to go to. A large workforce was needed to be able to run the machines and do the physical and mental work required to produce goods. One of the first management consultants of the time was Fredrick Taylor who, in 1911, wrote his infamous book *The Principles of Scientific Management.* In this he advocated training the workforce by detailed instruction and supervision of each worker. This became the 'go to' manual for anyone wanting to grow their business to the next level. His book became one of the leading management textbooks that reigned supreme for over 50 years with managers doing the thinking and workers doing the working.

For many people working in these factories provided them with a steady wage and the ability to purchase goods that were not just necessities, but luxuries. Economic cycles came and went, as well as the World Wars, and the industrial age continued with factories providing a source of employment for millions of people. More importantly, it gave people a sense of pride in creating something. They could finish a day's work at the factory and see the tangible results of their efforts, whether it was building cars or television sets.

It is important to remember that this gave people a sense of purpose – they knew their work was achieving something. Many of them would not make a big wage, but could see the fruits of their labour as well as provide for their family. I believe that this also started to fulfil the need for self-esteem. There is something built into our psyche that means earning an honest day's living is mentally soothing.

As globalization began in the 1980s, the manufacturing base shifted from the United States and Europe to Asia. As these new geographic territories opened up they were able to provide the same manufacturing at a fraction of the cost due to lower wages. This forced the traditional manufacturing companies to increase their efficiency, increase their product line or diversify into other industries.

It also led to the shedding and downsizing of hundreds of thousands of middle level staff. The mandate was to find a way to reduce overheads and costs in order to survive. But what did the people who lost their jobs do? They started up their own companies, often providing the same product or service at a reduced cost because they had fewer overheads and could move quicker than their former employers.

Thus began the next age for Western society – the information age with new industries starting up that had shifted away from physical labour to providing services, information and technology.

In his groundbreaking book, *The World is Flat: The globalized world in the twenty-first century*, Thomas Friedman tracked how this shift occurred. He identified the 10 forces that he believes made the world seem a much smaller place to live in including: computer software, uploading, outsourcing, off-shoring and supply chaining. However, the real change he believes occurred in the convergence of three specific events.

The first was the creation of technology that allowed for communication and collaboration across geographical borders and allowed people to take advantage of outsourcing simple tasks to other parts of the globe to increase efficiency and turnaround time. This could be through one of their parent companies, other office locations or subcontracting the work to someone who required a lower wage than a full-time employee.

The second event was the use of new technological products that allowed for the integration of hardware and software. Think about the days when you walked into an office that had an array of data processing machines for different purposes. Each computer would often have a separate printer, fax machine and scanner. With the integration of new hardware and software, products such as the multi-function printer was created – all of these activities in one machine and all linked via cable to everyone in the office.

The third convergence event Friedman identified was the opening of new markets and workforces being released from Communism. This provided a massive, willing workforce of over 3 billion people who actively wanted to earn a wage that would give them the same benefits as the American free market economy. The political and economic systems of countries such as China, India, Russia, Eastern Europe, Latin and Central America were opening up. The timing was perfect to take advantage of the new technologies that crossed geographical borders. Anyone with a computer and access to the internet could set up their own small business without a big investment to get started and sell products, services or ideas in the information age.

So what?

Conditions in the workforce are now very different from even twenty years ago. Work security has been reduced as companies go offshore and outsource their services. Automation and robotics are taking over the physical roles that provided an income for less well-educated and unskilled workers.

As society has changed, the basic needs that Maslow identified are now seen as an expectation, if not a right. In the Western world, governments provide most of the survival and security needs for the population through national social security programs, which help people who cannot find gainful employment. Many nations also provide basic health care to their citizens either through their employers or a nationalised medical safety net.

The ability to connect and have a sense of belonging is also being provided (especially to the younger generations) though the various forms of social media. People do not need to leave their home to connect with others, in fact, they can order almost any goods or services online and have them delivered without having to set foot outside their front door.

The problem now is what happens when people are unable to fulfil their higher level needs. What happens to someone who is unemployed and inactive? How are their needs for self-esteem met – and at what cost to society?

Without worthwhile work, we could be faced with a tsunami of societal ailments. We all agree there has been a significant increase in mental illness. Without having a sense of purpose or work, this worrying trend will only continue.

Creating and having worthwhile work is critical. We need to ensure that organizations design jobs that give a sense of accomplishment. Being realistic, few jobs will be perfect all the time, but they do have to provide the opportunity for workers to stretch, grow, create, learn, and make things happen. Workers also need to find ways to make their work more fulfilling, to see and appreciate what they are doing and look for opportunities to grow to the next level.

More importantly, they will also need to be aware of the order in which they are doing things. When at work and interacting with colleagues, the biggest impact is often not in *what* you do and say, but in *how* you do it and say it. We need to be more aware of what we are doing to assist others to grow and find fulfilment in the workplace. If all staff work towards creating an environment where everyone's work is appreciated and valued, a more positive culture will exist. The focus on results will remain, but the way we work with others to get these results will be what inspires us and demonstrates true greatness.

What are you doing to create work that is worth doing?

When was the last time you listened to your inner vision and acknowledged a colleague for the work they were doing?

How often do you think about the order or sequence you are going to use when asking for something from someone else? Does your approach encourage a sense of work worth doing?

Chapter 6

Mapping the Order: Practical business strategies

I believe that there are numerous ways for businesses and organizations to get their Sacred Order right. In fact, given the increase in competition, rapid growth in technology and new start-up businesses, the changing needs of the workforce must be a crucial component of your strategy.

Mapping the critical path forward will separate the companies that succeed from those that fail. Organizations that get their order right and create the right culture with worthwhile work will continue to excel and adapt. Leaders who shift their focus from 'what will I get?' to 'what can I give?' and 'how will I give it?' will continue to earn the admiration and commitment of their staff.

The Sacred Order for each organization is different. The required sequence needs to be adapted to the specific situation every time. Unfortunately, there is no management text book to provide your organization with the critical path of what needs to be done and how it needs to be done. This is something that you have to actively identify and share across your workforce.

I have often seen this in the numerous organizations I have worked with. I recall, in the mid-1990s, working as a full-time Learning and Development Manager with a company that had five manufacturing plants and had successfully supplied steel parts to American automotive manufacturers for years. Now all the manufacturers had embarked on rationalisation programs to reduce the number of their suppliers by more than half. This meant the very existence of the company I worked for was in jeopardy.

As a leadership team we recognized that, if we did not change the way we operated, our workforce of almost 600 would lose their jobs. Fortunately, we had a visionary owner and CEO who became very clear on getting the Sacred Order right. Specifically, he followed a critical path strategy that included five main components that clarified and communicated the vision, shifted the structure to reward and recognition of performance and found ways to promote successes internally and externally.

Actual Critical Path Manufacturing Company

Order	Focus
1	Shift the Vision & Management Mindset
2	Communicated & Engaged Staff with New Approach
3	Developed Business Units to Improve
4	Created a Profit Sharing & Recognition Program
5	Actively Promoted Shifts & Successes

Step #1: Shift the vision and managements mindset

The first initiative was to get very clear that the way forward was to change the way the business operated, by implementing the concept of New Shop Floor Management. This essentially turned the organization upside down and got the staff on the manufacturing line to start operating as mini-business owners.

It started with the management team being made aware of the need to change and take responsibility for the survival and success of the company. It also involved increasing their awareness and improving how they communicated, motivated and worked with the staff. Many of these managers had worked their way up the corporate ladder by following Frederick Taylor's philosophy of 'managers as thinkers' and 'workers as doers', so this was a big change. Fortunately most of them recognized that if this shift did not happen, they would need to look for new employment.

There were numerous discussions and a great deal of worry and uncertainty about how to make this change. However, the fact that everyone was in the same situation, provided a compelling reason to start doing things differently.

Step #2: Communicate and engage staff with a new approach

Once the management understood what they needed to start doing, the next step was to get all the staff involved. I personally conducted over 50 workshops on the need to change. These started with an initial three-hour session showing why we had to change and, more importantly, how we were going to change. The participants were a mixture of machine operators, maintenance staff, front-line supervisors, departmental managers and executive team members.

I can vividly remember one session when I was drawing a diagram showing how the traditional company pyramid would need to be flipped on its head with staff making decisions and leading the way. Upon hearing this, most of the employees looked directly at the managers to see if they believed this message too.

In the past it had not been uncommon for a worker sharing ideas with their peers to be shot down by their manager asserting their need for control. Now staff were looking for signs of support and commitment to this new approach. It was as if they were reading the concentric rings or energy to see if the managers really believed in this new approach. This is why I had lobbied for managers to be present at every session. Many of them participated in four or five sessions to demonstrate their support. By just showing up and being involved, they sent the message that they cared and had committed to the change that was about to occur.

We followed this up with another session to gather ideas and develop a framework for working in a new way. It was not always easy – many were stuck in old mindsets and approaches and there was a great deal of debate about how to proceed. However, because of the high level of staff participation and engagement in the methodology we used to focus on the 'why' for the change, as well as their awareness of the consequences of not changing, these issues were resolved.

It was not uncommon for staff to return to the assembly line with a buzz and a spring in their step. In fact, many managers noticed a lift in productivity and efficiency after the sessions.

Because staff were involved and participating in their future, they were experiencing first-hand work worth doing.

Step #3: Develop business units to improve

The sessions also involved the integration of new business practices, which were to turn the traditional linear assembly line into a business unit. One of the challenges in any manufacturing assembly process is ensuring high quality products are being produced. This can be tricky because each section of an assembly line builds upon the work completed by the previous section. This can lead to passing on the blame when issues with quality occur – a common approach that keeps people on autopilot and content with their current practices, rather than actively looking for ways to improve.

We implemented business units that took control of their area of operation. The operational KPIs (Key Performance Indicators) were shared and the business units could determine these targets and the initiatives needed to achieve them. Staff became involved in the scheduling of work hours, workflow planning and the continuous improvement process. More importantly, they also started to be exposed to the financial details of budgets, which gave them a stronger sense of ownership because they could see how that influenced the results.

We were based just outside Detroit, and most manufacturing plants in the region had a union competing with the management for control and protection of workers. This was necessary as the safety and mistreatment of workers in some plants was appalling. However, because our company operated in a consultative way, there was only one union in one of the five plants – a plant that had been purchased about 18 months earlier. Unfortunately, the union fought against this new approach and the effort to change the culture was too difficult.

As the other plants started turning things around, earnings jumped to about twice that of the unionised plant staff. As word spread, the union workers wanted the same opportunity, but the union contracts prevented this coordinated approach. Many workers transferred to other plants and, after a couple of weeks, realised they did not need a union because of the way the plant operated with their involvement – almost unheard of in the manufacturing world.

Step #4: Create a profit-sharing and recognition program

The most obvious goal was to ensure the company's survival as a preferred supplier to its major customers. This required an increase in efficiency, a decrease in waste and an increase in profit. In fact, there was a belief that, if we increased profits to a high enough level, we could share some with the staff, which would result in a stronger and more productive workforce.

This was implemented through a program called 'gain sharing'. In a traditional company this is when shares of stock are allocated to employees as a reward for reaching performance targets. As ours was a private company, the gain sharing was more of a financial profit share. Business units that achieved targets were rewarded with financial incentives.

The gain share bonus for one of our smaller plants, a tool and die factory that made specialty tools, meant every employee in this business unit received a quarterly bonus of almost $4,000. This was a significant amount for a worker who made an average annual salary of $35,000. It was almost double what they would normally earn in a month.

In an interesting shift, the rewards for the managers were also brought in line with the front-line staff. The management team would not receive their bonus unless their business units achieved their performance targets. This shifted the managers' focus from command and control to a philosophy of 'how can I help?' Managers now fully appreciated that their incentives were based on their ability to get the best out of their teams, shifting their goal from short term to long term to sustain results. The targets were not always reached because they were set to ensure that workers had to make an effort to lift their performance.

We created a culture worth belonging to. Staff could not only gain fulfilment from their work, they could also see they would be rewarded for working together to achieve results. We also put reward programs in place to provide smaller forms of recognition. We installed continuous improvement suggestion boxes and a committee of front-line staff and managers analysed the suggestions and those that helped improve performance or operating conditions were rewarded.

Once the first person at one of the plants was recognized for submitting a continuous improvement idea with a $500 voucher for a weekend away, we were flooded with suggestions.

Everyone wanted a chance to be rewarded. After we received a few recommendations to change the colour of the toilet paper from white to blue, we provided some guidelines for future suggestions!

The small forms of recognition ranged from weekends away to movie tickets, meal vouchers and other gift packs. This helped to keep the momentum going when the larger business unit targets were difficult to achieve as steel prices rose or when transportation costs increased due to a rise in diesel prices. It was often these little rewards that people remembered.

Step #5: Actively promote shifts and successes

Another key activity was to increase the promotion of achievements and challenges overcome across the manufacturing plants. This was not a natural habit for this world and there had to be an entirely new way of thinking. Previously, there was a factory full of machines that turned steel into parts. The workers' entire focus was on production and their immediate machine or plant line. Now the new focus was on promoting how this smaller company could compete on a national level and proudly display these improvements and results.

I can remember watching the manager who was in charge of quality control promoting the increase in efficiencies to customers who were on a site inspection. He proudly showed them the business units and the visual control boards the front-line workers updated and tracked during their shift. The staff would look on with pride because they could see the recognition and appreciation the manager was giving them, often calling out to them by name in front of the customers.

The annual picnic for staff and their families to celebrate the successes of the past year and recognize staff who achieved incredible results, was an event not to be missed because it provided a chance to meet with co-workers. It gave them a sense of belonging that felt more like a family than a company. The managers served the food to all of the guests, as well as participating in games designed to allow people to play together and have fun outside the workplace.

By following this sequence we were able not only to lift performance and profits, but the company was able to keep their top tier supplier status with their major customers. Their future in a changing industry was assured. What made this possible? The Order. By completing the steps in this sequence, the workforce was empowered to make a shift towards the new vision and stayed focused on the critical path.

The biggest mistake I see many companies making is they do things in the wrong sequence. When this happens things can go wrong – and often do. Staff become disillusioned, managers get frustrated, communication breaks down and even simple tasks become difficult.

So, what is the critical path for your organization? What Sacred Order should your leaders be implementing on a daily basis? By focusing on your strategy and getting your hierarchy right you can empower your workforce and achieve incredible results. Business can probably continue along as normal, but given the amount of disruption and emerging technologies, organizations that take this approach may be operating on borrowed time.

Practical Exercise.

Capture what the Sacred Order should be for your organization. What should be the most important focus given the current need and situation?

Do you have a culture worth belonging to? How do you know? What rating would you give the current culture on a scale from 1 to 10 (with 1 being the lowest and 10 being the highest)? What criteria are you using to score them this way? Would all of your staff agree? Is there anything missing?

Are your leaders on their critical path? Do they follow a philosophy or approach that ensures they create a workforce that believes it has leaders worth following? If not, why not, and what needs to change?

How fulfilled are your employees? Do they have the sense that they are involved in work worth doing or are they just going through the motions, collecting a pay cheque and looking for another job that will light them up? What could be done to shift this so they have the opportunity to be challenged, grow and participate?

Specific business critical pathways

I am often asked to provide examples of how organizations and leaders have mapped out their order or sequence to allow them to start progressing towards their critical path. Although the specific details depend on the situation and people involved, there are a number of critical pathways that I have found to be useful for many leaders.

In mapping these critical pathways, I have also noticed that there are usually five to seven milestones or touchpoints that comprise the higher order of what to do. The details and specifics generally fill out around this framework and make it easier to see and act on the way forward.

I want to provide a few examples of what the order looks like and a brief description of how to go about doing the right things, at the right time, in the right way. Please feel free to adapt this to assist you in building a stronger company culture that empowers staff with work worth doing and leaders worth following.

The critical path to delegate to others

Most managers do not know how to delegate. They think that just telling one of their staff to do a specific task will achieve the results they are looking for and they are often disappointed. We have seen how previous generations of managers bought into Fredrick Taylor's philosophy that staff should not do any thinking, but wait to be told what to do and how to do it. This is completely out of step with the way things need to be done today.

So how can you delegate in a way that gets staff committed enough that they want to do it and own it as if it was their idea? The Delegation Model provides a framework of understanding around how you can effectively delegate in a clear way that empowers staff and achieves results.

Critical Path to Effective Delegation

Order	Focus
1	Identify Task & Who to Delegate it to
2	Map the Steps Together
3	Identify the Sequence of Steps
4	Identify Check-in Deadlines & Let them Lead
5	Check-in, Support & Accountability

Step 1. Identify the task and who to delegate it to

This first step and highest level order is to identify what can be delegated. Everyone knows that a manager cannot possibly complete all the tasks of their department themselves, but this does not stop them from trying. Too often experienced managers do not delegate tasks to others for two common reasons: time and control.

Firstly, they falsely believe they can do the task more quickly themselves rather than taking the time to explain to one of their subordinates what they want done and how they want it done. This may be true at first, but if the task needs to be repeated, the manager will again have to invest this time. The staff member is also missing out on an opportunity to grow and be challenged with new initiatives – which is a key ingredient of having work worth doing.

The second reason that managers do not delegate is that they are afraid of putting their reputation, their KPIs and their performance objectives in the hands of someone else. They can have difficulty sharing control with others. This is especially the case with people who have a tendency to be perfectionists and believe that no one can do things as well as they can. This delusion often results in the manager being overwhelmed and isolated from their staff as they scramble to complete tasks they should not be doing because they are taking them away from doing the important things that need to be done.

Once you have identified a task to delegate, you need to identify who to delegate the task to. You can select the candidate based on their knowledge, skills or experience. You can also make a selection based on their motivation and willingness to be challenged and stretched.

Once you have decided, rather than telling the person that they need to do something, the best way to start is to ask them for their help in developing a strategy to complete the task. By shifting the approach from telling to asking, the relationship dynamics change from a traditional top-down approach to one that puts them on more even footing. You are asking them to get involved *with* you – rather than doing something *for* you.

Step 2. Map the steps together

After you have identified the task and who to delegate to, you need to work together with that person to map the possible actions to completing the task. To start this process it is useful to ask them a question about what they think some of the required initiatives or actions are. This encourages them to share their insights with you and allows you to understand their current ability to problem solve and the methodology they use for their reasoning. Either way you are strengthening the relationship and increasing the chances of success.

The key is to map it visually with them so both of you can see the possible steps or tasks being considered. As they share an idea or possible action to take, create a mind map on a sheet of paper so both of you can see what you are discussing. This allows you to refer back to the previous steps if you get stuck or you need to merge a few ideas. Ideally, you will be mentoring them – drawing out their ideas rather than just telling them the steps to take and writing them down.

In my experience if you can keep the number of initiatives or steps to between five and seven, you will increase their focus and chance for success. Any more than this can become overly complex and create confusion. The aim is to empower and encourage them to step up and develop a strategy to do something that they may not have done before.

Step 3. Identify the sequence of steps

After identifying the steps or initiatives, determine the sequence or order they need to be taken in to complete the task. This is one of the most important stages and is typically overlooked when people delegate. Remember to ask them what they believe the order should be and help mentor them along the way.

This process allows staff to build their understanding and skill base. It requires a higher level of problem solving because people need to have the ability to rank priorities. This process also allows the manager to teach and mentor them in these areas. If they make a mistake and mix up the sequence, provide guidance towards the preferred order and the reasoning behind it so they understand why.

I find just writing the number of the sequence next to the actions on the sheet of paper you have been working on is the easiest method to use. I always use different coloured pens to capture the sequence and make it stand out visually on the paper. Any assistance to enhance this stage is important because this is going to be what they follow to ensure that they get the order right and complete the task.

Many managers who have followed this Delegation Model have commented on how often they are surprised by what they learnt about their staff. Although some of their staff had been in a role for years, their ability to problem solve and think for themselves was limited. After taking this approach, they gained a fuller understanding of the true capabilities of their people. By working alongside their staff they discovered untapped skills and abilities that were overlooked or unnoticed in their everyday role.

Step 4. Identify the check-in deadlines and let them lead

Most tasks that are delegated will have a number of steps to be completed along the way. To ensure that they feel supported, and are held accountable, a number of one-on-one check-ins and deadlines should be scheduled. Usually there is a timeframe within which the entire task needs to be complete and linking timeframes to the agreed steps or milestones identified is a good rule of thumb.

So, assuming that a task has six steps that need to be completed, you may assign a check-in at steps number two and four. Set a time and date and the place to meet. The amount of time between the check-ins will be influenced by the size and timeframe for the entire task. Once again, I recommend putting this check-in timeframe on the same sheet of paper you have been using to show these deadlines next to the agreed order of actions.

Another useful strategy is to encourage them take the sheet of paper on which you have mapped the task. This physical document will give them a sense of ownership and be a reminder of the plan you developed together. I also recommend taking a digital photo of the written plan. This lets them know you have a copy of the plan to be used as a back-up resource. Gone are the days when 'My dog ate it' or 'I cannot find the paper' can be used as an excuse. In addition, with so many things on their plate, a busy manager may also need a method of recalling what was discussed and agreed to days, or even weeks, earlier.

After providing them with the plan, the next step is to let them take the lead. They have the plan, an understanding of how to go about the plan and timeframes for check-ins and completion. Your role as manager is to support them along the way. While you do not want to ignore them and be invisible once they have their plan, you also do not want to micromanage everything. By being visible and around, it makes it easier for them to ask you any follow-up questions or share new thoughts or insights with you. Once they start to take action, it is important to honour the check-in timeframes you have agreed to and give them the opportunity to take action.

Step 5. Check-in, support and accountability

As your first check-in nears, remind them of the commitment that you both made and the actions they agreed to take before the first deadline. This lets them know you have not forgotten about the task they have been working on. If you are working in the same place, you can go to their desk area or a neutral spot for the check-in, showing them that you are supporting them, rather than them having to report back to you. If necessary, it is easy to have a video call on Skype, Google Hangouts or your organization's internal video conferencing platform so you can see each other face to face.

The check-in is now simply a matter of them providing you with an update on the actions they have taken. Ideally they would have produced some sort of evidence of activity that you can see. If you have come across a new piece of relevant information, share this with them so they can integrate it into their next steps.

If for some reason they have not taken action, then you need to hold them accountable. The beauty of this process is that you can refer to the copy of the plan you both created and ask them why they chose not to take action. They may say they didn't have time or that they were too busy, but this should not just be accepted automatically. When you agreed to the timeframes, hopefully workloads were considered.

A useful strategy if this occurs is to let them know you have also been busy but made time to check in with them. Ask them what they think they need to do to make up the time to get the tasks done before the next check-in – especially if the deadline cannot be changed. It is not about getting angry, but about understanding why they did not follow through. There is nothing wrong with people being held accountable and experiencing some discomfort if they have let you down. In fact, most people will be motivated to ensure it doesn't happen again. If their deadline has slipped, you may need to assist them in rearranging what they are currently doing with their time to get this back on track.

Holding them accountable in a supportive way will make most staff appreciate the relationship even more. Most people look forward to being stretched and challenged in new ways as it provides them with work worth doing. This is true as long as the order their manager uses builds the relationship, rather than destroying it.

The delegation model with a modification

There are also a few modifications to this Delegation Model that can be used after someone you have been working with is familiar with the process of visually mapping out the steps with you.

Once you have used this approach three or four times, most people will be able to mind map a task themselves. Encourage them to identify the actions, the sequence and the check-in timeframes. This is demonstrating that you have faith in their capabilities and that you value their contribution, which in turn strengthens your relationship with them. Get them to show you their mind map and ask them questions to ensure you fully understand their plan and provide any necessary recommendations that can make their implementation of the plan more efficient. Not only does this develop their skills and capabilities further, it also will start saving your time. The more they invest in developing their plan, the more time you have for your tasks – you begin to act as a mentor who reviews and recommends, rather than someone who has to always have complete control.

The Critical Path to Improving Team Spirit

One of my tasks is to show how to improve team spirit or the sense of commitment to a common goal at a departmental level. I often draw on the research from my Master's thesis on teams and blend this with native wisdom to provide insights. There is a natural order that can be followed and allows you to adapt the specifics based on your people, your purpose and the outcome you are after.

Critical Path to Improving Team Spirit

Order	Focus
1	Clarify Need for Team Spirit/Re-identify Purpose of Team
2	Internalize the Purpose of the Team
3	Align Each Team Member
4	Establish Agreed Touchpoints
5	Recognize Action and Reward & Celebrate Success

Step 1. Clarify need for team spirit and re-identify the purpose of the team

The first step is to take a look at why the team spirit needs to be improved. A common reason is that a high degree of change has occurred and individual team members (or the manager) are feeing disconnected, leading to a drop in team morale. Another reason may be that performance has become inconsistent and the team could benefit from having a collective approach.

One common technique is to survey the team members and ask them a series of questions to identify what is not working to the level it should. The survey could also include a number of specific questions around team spirit and asking individuals to score the current level on a scale of 1 to 10 (with 1 being low and 10 being excellent). These surveys can provide a baseline you can check against by re-measuring over time to track your progress.

Once you have identified the reason for the drop in team spirit, it is important to re-identify and re-establish the purpose of the team. Why does the team exist and what is its primary objective? You can also take a look at how achieving or not achieving this goal impacts on other departments, the organization and any potential customers.

Ideally this is done with the team members so they can identify and appreciate how they affect other parts of the business. Sometimes gaining this perspective is enough to get people to recognize the work they are doing does make a difference, even it if is repetitive and not perceived as a glamorous or high profile function.

Step 2. Internalise the purpose of the team

Once the team is aware of the difference they make externally, identify the difference they can make internally. Look for interactions of support, belonging and encouragement that have demonstrated this sense of connection and team spirit in the past.

Encourage the team to identify its own vision and how it wants to function and operate. Look at how you can link the operational KPIs to this internal vision so people will be able to appreciate how their activity supports the team and helps achieve the team spirit you are aiming for.

I worked with one government team responsible for managing dam infrastructure and engineering upgrades across the state. This group of highly technical and skilled engineers could benefit from working together and creating a spirit of camaraderie. Once they came together they realised the potential that they had internally and externally.

They started monthly sharing updates to brainstorm difficult engineering challenges and established an internal blog to post questions and share ideas. They created their own vision for their skills and capabilities to be recognized not just across the organization, but across the state. An internal team plan was developed around this purpose and they were quickly noticed to be operating at a higher collective level than most of the other departments.

When the state government decided to amalgamate two government agencies into one, theirs was the one recognized as leading the way. The other department was folded into their structure with minimal disruption so they sustained their core functions and achieved the kind of results they were known for. Many of the managers were selected to run other departments and a few were headhunted by outside firms because of their reputation. This did not create a problem in their department because the assistant manager was able to step up on the strong foundation they had helped create and the transition from one manager to the next was more effective.

Step 3. Align each team member

The team's collective departmental vision then needs to be adapted to the individual level i.e. aligned to each team member. They need to know what it means for them – what they need to give and what they will get from committing to the team and operating on this level.

This is a personal and specific approach. With one particular sales team we took the overall team targets and broke these down into individual targets, letting people see how their individual commitment helped the team achieve its goals. Each person was aligned with the individual sales target they needed to reach each month.

More importantly, we worked with individual sales consultants and asked them to state their salary targets for the year. We identified this figure based on the income they wanted to make and aligned that back to the team's goal to ensure a good fit. We also asked them why they wanted to make this income and what they would do with the income they made above the previous year.

This allowed them to set goals that had real meaning to them – personal and tangible outcomes rather than just an amount of money. Some personal goals included taking their family on a week's holiday overseas or renovating a bathroom or kitchen. When they had this as their personal vision, they were even more committed and aligned to achieving these results. They also appreciated the impact and support of other team members in reaching the overall team goal as well as their own personal goals. In fact, many of them wanted to assist other team members reach their chosen desires as well as their own.

Step 4. Establish agreed touchpoints

Once individual goals are agreed on, it is important to establish touchpoints to ensure that individuals continue to actively and consistently build up the team camaraderie.

These touchpoints, or activities, can be anything that will ensure the team continues to work together. One of the most important parts of this step is to identify the expectations each team member has. By allowing people to share what they do and do not want to occur starts to establish an agreed framework. Additional touchpoints could include setting up monthly team meetings (as long as they are effective), departmental performance updates and identifying behavioural KPIs on how they are going to treat and interact with one another.

Team-building events that allow each member to get to know, understand and appreciate other team members free from day-to-day work requirements can also be beneficial. Taking time to play together provides the opportunity to see others in a different perspective when not confined to their everyday role.

It can also be valuable to reassess the level of team spirit over time. Revisiting the initial team baseline set at the very beginning of the process can provide an update on progress. This can also be used to address the situation when agreed touchpoints are being ignored or overlooked.

Step 5. Recognize action and reward and celebrate success

The final step, and one not to forget, is to find ways to recognize action and initiatives that support both the collective purpose and individual performance. Giving appropriate recognition that works for the team and for the individual is important.

I have experienced many team celebrations in which someone was unintentionally made extremely uncomfortable because they did not enjoy being singled out in front of their peers. For some people, forcing them to parade around in front of others for a job well done is worse than speaking in public or going to the dentist.

Make sure that the recognition and rewards are relevant and valuable to the people receiving them. Making a big deal out of a $10 fuel voucher may actually demotivate the person receiving it as well as the rest of the team because they may view it as an insult. Ask staff what they feel would be an appropriate reward and find ways to make it happen.

I also recommend, if possible, providing rewards an employee can share with their spouse or family. Imagine the impact when someone receives a weekend away at a nice hotel for them and their family as a reward for achieving a high level of success. Not only will the employee feel appreciated, their family feels appreciated – and will encourage them to continue their efforts to be rewarded again!

By using this simple order to improve team spirit you can implement an approach that creates cultures worth belonging to within departments. There are numerous ways you can adapt the steps to add your own team's personality and objectives.

Chapter 7

Fast Track Tables of Critical Paths for Business

To provide you with a further reference, I wanted to share with you a table of useful critical paths in business. Please feel free to modify and adapt these to further enhance your organization, your leaders and your people.

Critical Path to improve team spirit
Critical Path to improve customer service
Critical Path to a sales call
Critical Path to building individual capability
Critical Path to give feedback
Critical Path to writing a speech
Critical Path to organizing a conference
Critical Path to run an effective team meeting
Critical Path to interview a potential employee
Critical Path to teaching staff to sell

Note: Each of these Paths will have 5 steps that will be listed to show the order to be followed.

Critical Path to improve team spirit

Order	Focus
1	Clarify need for team spirit/re-identify purpose of team
2	Internalize the purpose of the team
3	Align each team member
4	Establish agreed touchpoints
5	Recognize action and reward & celebrate success

Critical Path to improve customer service

Order	Focus
1	Identify customer touchpoints and customer expectations
2	Identify activities to meet customer expectations
3	Identify possible "wow" activities to exceed
4	Analyse the cost/benefit of recommendations
5	Implement and track

Critical Path to a sales call

Order	Focus
1	Start by thanking them and stating purpose of meeting
2	Ask questions to understand who they are and their need
3	Provide overview of your offer: Educate and inform
4	Communicate how your offer fills their need
5	Ask for the sale

Critical Path to building individual capability

Order	Focus
1	Identify task/skill/ability to improve
2	Together map the steps or requirements to task
3	You show/demonstrate task with them watching
4	They try whilst you watch and you coach
5	They implement and you check over time for ability

Critical Path to give feedback

Order	Focus
1	Start by reflecting on any positive activity
2	Map what you see and issues occurring with them (ideally on paper)
3	Ask them to understand their perspective
4	Identify alternatives together
5	Agree to new approach, document and thank them

Critical Path to writing a speech

Order	Focus
1	Identify your objective & why someone should listen
2	Map the Main Points
3	Add Stories and Examples to bring it to life
4	Add introduction and Conclusion & Sequence the Order
5	Practice Presenting

Critical Path to organizing a conference

Order	Focus
1	Set topic & theme
2	Identify dates and location
3	Identify agenda, sessions and speakers
4	Promote to participants/Registration
5	Identify the pre-conference and post-conference touchpoints

Critical Path to run an effective team meeting

Order	Focus
1	Start with objectives and outcomes of meeting
2	Quick check-in on wins and challenges
3	Explore agenda items and discuss
4	Identify action plans & accountability (who, what, when)
5	Communication plan of meeting outcomes (tell what to who, how and by when)

Critical Path to interview a potential employee

Order	Focus
1	Provide vision of organisation and overview of role
2	Ask them why this job/role?
3	Interview questions using S.T.A.R. (situation, task, actions, results) Method
4	Provide them with role related tasks to complete/ demonstrate capability or potential
5	Clarify any of their questions and inform them of next steps

Critical Path to teaching staff to sell

Order	Focus
1	Educate about product and marketplace
2	Map ideal sales process, KPI activity & skills needed
3	Educate/train staff in process, KPI activity & skills
4	Coach staff whilst they implement
5	Monitor activity & recognise effort

Section 4

Life Critical Pathways

Life is supposed to be about more than just work. We know this, we just forget it from time to time. So how can you stay true to your path? What can you do to keep your order right so that you do the right things at the right time in the right way?

Many people have mixed up their life and work order so much that they are completely off path. A number of years ago I worked with a very senior executive for one of the largest investment banks in Australia. He was considered a very high flyer and was well known for his success and the money he made – he earned over $1million a year.

I was asked to work with him and his sales team because their performance had gone off course and they wanted to identify how to refocus and return to their normal performance level. I first met with him in the executive meeting room. As I walked in, I noticed he was looking me over from head to toe. From his attitude, I knew he was judging my wealth and expertise based on what I was wearing. He was not impressed. He sat back in his chair and looked down at me.

I explained I was there to ask him a few questions in order to understand how the team operated. I praised his success and the incredible results he had achieved in the last couple of years at the bank. I then asked him one simple question: 'Why?' He looked at me as if I was from another planet and said; 'What do you mean, "why?"' I replied, 'What motivated you to want to work the hours you did to make the money you have?'

He shifted in his chair and gave me the typical response – he wanted to be successful and earn a great living. I simply nodded and asked him the same question: 'So why did you want this?' He suddenly realised the real question I was asking. His energy began to shift and the colour drained from his face as he looked at me and said, 'Well, I guess when I first started with the bank we had only been married for about five or six years and our kids were younger and I wanted us to have a nice house and be able to get the kids into good schools and be able to go on family holidays together.'

As he spoke these words, he suddenly stopped talking and slowly bowed his head. I could see tears start to form in his eyes. 'I just don't know what happened. My wife left me a year ago and the kids don't want to know me.' As he started to cry he looked me in the eyes and said, 'If I could give anything to go back in time I would. I'd give away the millions I have made just to get back to how it was.'

He was a lost soul who had chased the dream that money can buy happiness. He had sacrificed it all for a myth. When he finally attained the money, he realised he had left behind the very people he wanted to share it with and he was now all alone. He had lost what was important to him and gone completely off his critical path.

Apache elder Stalking Wolf believed that many white people had a disease. He watched as people turned away from the wisdom of the ages and embraced what he called the 'gods of the flesh'. As they chased material goods, he saw them become more and more isolated from what is real. Of course, during the early 1950s, life was much simpler and, as someone who was raised to live off the land, he had a greater understanding of how all things are interconnected. He saw how the vast prairies were carved up and large highway systems built so we could drive our cars from place to place. He watched as the modern world built more and more ways to separate us from the real world.

I believe that we need to go back to the basics. We need to strip off all the artificial layers we put over our true soul and start living the way we know we should. We need to have courage to follow our inner vision and become the person we are destined to be. For some this is a complete 180 degree turnaround from the way they currently live their life. Many have lost their way and are off their path. In an attempt to keep 'positive' they put on a fake smile and focus on their appearance. They surround themselves with material things to increase their perceived status in society. It is frightening to think how many people are living beyond their means and accumulate material goods to feed their desire to keep up with their friends.

We now live insulated lives and watch the world through our windows – for many this means on television. We regulate temperature with artificial air to keep our environment consistent. Our bare feet rarely touch the earth because of the cement footpaths and we always wear shoes for fear of stepping on something that will harm us. It is almost as if we have tried to isolate ourselves and our children from what is real.

I grew up in America in the 1970s and the images of the Vietnam war were fresh in my memory. Being an adventure guide leading a 30-day cycling trip through Vietnam in the mid-1990s, was an eye-opening experience for me. Communist Vietnam had just started allowing a few tourist in. The country was beautiful and no matter where we went, the people always waved and smiled at us.

One of our rest days was spent in the beautiful seaside village of Hoi An. There I met a 20-year-old Vietnamese girl. Our riding group wearing skin-tight lycra cycling shorts though her village made her curious. She asked me what life was like in Australia and America.

I tried to tell her what a typical day was for many working people. They lived in apartment buildings full of individual units, many travelled to work in the morning by train or bus. They went to their office building in the city, rode up in an elevator to their floor and went to their office, or cubicle, to start work. Getting their work done usually involved using a computer and a phone as they typed on the keyboard, looked at the screen and spoke on the phone. In the middle of the day they went to the lunch room to eat. Some of the fancier lunch rooms had vending machines from which you could buy a box of soup or something you could heat up in a microwave. After work they caught the bus or train home and many would then go to a gym. These were quite modern, with treadmill machines that allowed people to run and watch television at the same time.

A very strange look crossed her face as if she did not understand something. Then she described the image she was seeing in her head. 'So people live in a unit that is a box that is inside an apartment building that is a bigger box. They ride in a box on wheels to work that is a square building and travel up the building in another box. When they get to their workplace it is like a small box inside the larger box. And when they eat they heat up a box in another electric box?'

'Yes,' I replied as I thought about her response. She giggled and said, 'And to stay in shape they go to another box, run on a machine indoors and watch another box? Why wouldn't they just go for a walk or a run outside to see the beauty that is in nature around them?' I suddenly realised what she was really saying. She could not believe that we had become so sterile that we had built an artificial environment to live in and completely ignored the natural world around us.

I have always been challenged by the idea that there are 52 weeks in the year and that we need to work for 48 of them (or 50 in the US!). Since I was young, this did not make sense to me. A common saying is: 'Do we live to work, or do we work to live?'

In the *New York Times* best-selling book *The 4-Hour Work Week,* Timothy Ferriss advocates finding a way to live a millionaire lifestyle by changing the way you view work and how you operate by focusing on the 20% of stuff that is important and eliminating the 80% that is not. As an entrepreneur, outsourcing menial tasks is a strategy he has used to create a lifestyle that balances both work and play. To explain what he did to achieve this, Ferriss has a range of recommendations from defining what is important to eliminating distractions and increasing your job mobility. Although his book targets the entrepreneur, it is relevant for anyone who needs another way of viewing how they work.

The reality for most of us is that we need to earn an income and we also want a life that is our own. How do we do both? How can you have a career that inspires you, balances the time you need to spend with your spouse or partner, kids, extended family, friends, the community and still lets you have time for you?

You need to make a conscious choice to take yourself off autopilot and get clear about what is important and what you really should be doing. It is actually a very simple decision to make if you are aware of a few important principles. These can be a personal guide for your life journey.

The Four Principles of Life Critical Pathways

- Who you are: your identity
- What you stand for: your beliefs
- Who you stand with: your tribe
- How you live: your concentric rings

Sacred Order in Life

Each of these principles can help guide you like a compass. It can help you find your true north and give you a bearing to refer to when needed. More importantly, it can help you stay true to your path and give you guidance on how to get your order right.

Chapter 1

Who You Are – Your identity

Who are you – really? This can be a confronting question because it forces you to take a look at what is really there. Have you ever looked at a photo that someone had taken of you and had the thought that the image doesn't quite match the one you had in your mind? You may look shorter/taller, fatter/skinnier, prettier/uglier, older/younger or just different. Most people have two different views of who they are: the external and the internal.

Our external identity

This is the one we project to the world around us. It is the image we want other people to see and how we want them to view us. It is often on the very surface of who we are or what we want others to think.

Most people have an idea of how they want others to view them – usually favourably – but they have not thought about it in any detail. Most of us can think of a number of virtues we would want other people to use to describe us – honest, trustworthy, a good person, friendly, fun to be around.

Another external identity most people refer to is their job title. When asked what they do, they respond with their role at work. Common categories used to include accountant, builder, project manager, cashier or garbage man. Now, in modern society, we have created new titles that sound more important. Josh Linkner wrote a great article, 'The 21 Most Creative Job Titles' for the December 2014 issue of *Forbes Magazine.* Some of the titles he found included: Director of First Impressions (receptionist); Crayon Evangelist (graphic designer); Genius (service technician – Apple retail stores); and Master of Disaster (disaster consultant).

Although these labels are easy for others to understand, it is important to remember that we are not what we do. We are much more.

Our internal identity

This is the way we view ourselves. It is mainly influenced by the voices we have in our head. Specifically, the mind that speaks to us in an unending stream of consciousness.

When we looked at the photo of ourselves, it is the voice that said, 'I look a lot older than I thought,' 'Is my hair really that grey?' or 'The next time I'm in a photo I need to make sure that I pose on my better side, and keep my head up so they can't see my double chin.' These thoughts provide us with a constant barrage of feedback that influences how we view ourselves. There are four levels we go through that shape our identity: experiences, feelings/emotions, meaning, and memory. Each of these is a distinct step that together determine the image we have of our self.

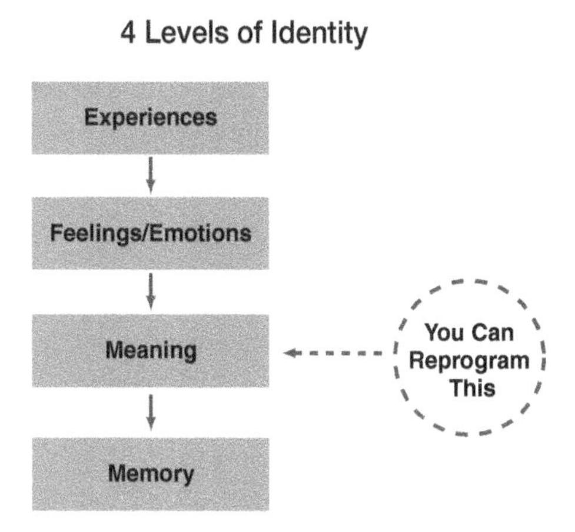

Our experiences

Or lives are filled with experiences – both good and bad. These ultimately shape who we are as a person. Think back to some of the ordinary experiences you have had. It may be the time you rode the bus to school for the first time and nobody would move over to allow you sit next to them. Or it could have been the first time you went out on a date with someone you really liked.

These moments in time are like a snapshot or video that captures the scene as it occurred. At this level, they are nothing more and nothing less than a record. What occurs at the next level is where we start shaping them.

Feelings/Emotions

Once we have an experience we unconsciously attach a feeling or an emotion to it ranging across a broad spectrum from the positive emotions of happiness, warmth, safety, love and invincibility to the negative emotions of pain, fear, anger and frustration. We also rate the intensity of the emotion from something almost non-existent to something so intense that when we think about it, even ten years later, we can still feel the emotion.

Meaning

From the combination of experience and our emotion we create meaning, as if our mind needs to organize these into categories that make sense to us. Our personal filters can often influence the meaning of the event.

I was an Operations Manager for a leadership and team building company based in Atlanta, Georgia, during the 1990s when outdoor team building was all the rage. As companies looked for ways to build their teams, they sent them outdoors for trust activities such as high ropes courses.

I was extremely stressed out because I had shipped the wrong team-building equipment to a program on the other side of the country, so there was no way to get the equipment needed on time the next day. I ran around in a panic and was naturally very upset I had let our staff down. I could not believe how I could have made such a big mistake and was mentally beating myself up over it.

I had an incredible boss – Andy 'studmuffin' Dishman – who helped me give new meaning to this experience. In his southern Alabama drawl he said, 'Scotty, nobody's perfect. Just do the best you can and move on. In fact, in two or three weeks, you will not even remember that you made this mistake, so why give it energy it doesn't deserve?' In that moment he showed me how I could change the meaning I had given to an experience – something I have never forgotten.

Memory

Once we have given an experience or event a meaning, we store it in our mind and remember the emotions we have placed on it. But, more importantly, the meanings that we hold influence and shape who we are – our identity.

If we place a large number of negative meanings and memories on past events, we remember the difficult things and this can affect the way we behave. We need to stop the negative influences arising from these experiences or we can become defensive and keep our guard up to protect ourselves from repeating them.

The same is true if we place a large number of positive meanings on past events. In essence, our memory programs us for who we are on a daily basis. It remembers our routine and automatically allows us to follow this, without requiring conscious thought or energy. It shapes the self-talk in our mind and the messages we send our self on a daily basis.

Why is this important?

When we know what has shaped our identity we can make the choice to be who we want to be. We can look at past experiences and change the meaning we held of it in our heads. We can turn it from a painful negative experience we are trying to forget to one that provides a valuable life lesson.

In many cases we can even reprogram our mind to give the experience a new meaning to replace the old own – an extremely helpful process to assist someone get past what is holding them back from being the person they are meant to be.

Dr Martin Seligman researched the internal voices people have in their heads for his groundbreaking book, *Learned Optimism*. Many of us have an orientation – negative or positive – that influences how we live our lives. Seligman found that people who have fallen into a pattern of pessimism often create a pattern of helplessness – they do not believe they have control over who they are, what they can do, or what else is possible. His research has proven that people can learn how to overcome these patterns and become more optimistic, allowing them to have greater fulfilment and success in life. In essence, this means you can reprogram the meaning you give experiences and this can turn the memory into something you can use to help you stay on path.

Your identity helps you to be clearer on what you should be doing and how you should be doing it. When times are challenging you can refer to who you are and use this to guide you.

Chapter 2

What You Stand For – Your beliefs

Identity is who you are and what you stand for are your beliefs. These are important because we accept them to be true and bigger than we are. Beliefs guide us towards what we see as right and can directly shape our future course.

Our beliefs are important because the way we think guides the way we behave. Sociologist Robert Merton created the phrase 'self-fulfilling prophecy' in an initial article he wrote for the *Antioch Review* and added further insights in his book *Social Theory and Social Structure.* A self-fulfilling prophecy is when someone believes something will happen so much they influence that outcome. If you believe something negative is about to occur, you look for anything negative and focus your mind on that to convince yourself it has occurred. A negative self-fulfilling prophecy can create limitations which influence you to start being pessimistic, which leads to helplessness. A positive self-fulfilling prophecy can actually have the opposite effect – we can shift our belief toward the positive things that are occurring and become more optimistic. Whether positive or negative, they both influence our mindset and behaviour.

There are two other important variables to be aware of in what you stand for: values and conviction.

Values

We all have values – principles or personal preferences. They are the things we believe are important in the way we work and the way we live, the higher beliefs we hold as extremely important in our lives.

Some common values include:

- Family
- Security
- Health
- Wealth
- Learning/Growth
- Independence
- Creativity
- Honesty
- Dependability

Many people also use their values to assess if they are living the life they want to live. Values can be used to 'track your signs' and as an internal check-in to make sure you are doing what you should be doing. However, we can be challenged when two or more of these values are tested at the same time.

Think of a time when you may have had to choose between two values: family and dependability. Perhaps you had to work back late on an important project so as not to let your colleagues down. At the same time one of your daughters had a dance recital. Which did you choose? We often have to make a selection that is not ideal – we want to do both and our values point us to do both.

Most people have a hierarchy of values, which can help in these situations as it allows them to rank one action over another. We do this unconsciously. In the scenario above some people would justify staying back for work to keep their job, which allows them to pay for their daughter's dance lessons, costume and recital. Some would decide to go to the recital and let their work colleagues complete the task. Either choice is a valid option.

There is a third option that many people overlook – finding a way to do both. Rather than ranking them in a hierarchy, you could actually do them in sequence allowing you to do both. After your normal work day, you attend your daughter's dance and when it is finished, you return to work and complete your important task. Yes, it would require extra effort, energy and organization, but by looking for alternatives we can try to find a way to satisfy both values. Although it may not work in every situation, we often need to look from a different perspective to be aware of other options.

Regardless of what values we have they are all important. They are the signposts of our lives that provide direction when we need it. They are often the voice of our inner vision sending messages about the path we should be travelling. We still have the choice to listen to our values or ignore them. How much we listen is often based on our conviction to a particular value.

Convictions

A conviction is a firmly held belief that we would be willing to stand up for – a deeply known truth we hold inside. We all have beliefs, but very few of us have the conviction to stand up for them. This takes more than knowing something to be true, it is the conscious acceptance of the need to act on that belief.

When I think of Rosa Parks, I think of someone who demonstrated the courage and conviction to stand up for what she believed in. Imagine what it would be like to grow up as a black woman in the deep south of America in the mid-1950s and be treated like a second-class citizen under Alabama's race segregation laws. These limited what black people could do based on the colour of their skin. They could not eat at the same counters in restaurants, they could not use the same toilets and they could not sit on the same seats on a bus as white people.

Rosa Parks made history on the 1 December 1955 when she demonstrated her conviction. The Montgomery City Code required that all public transport be segregated. Generally on buses this meant the front part of the bus was for white people and the back for coloured people. After working a long day as a seamstress, the bus started to fill up with passengers. When all the seats were full, there were white passengers standing in the aisle, so the bus driver stopped the bus and asked four black passengers to give up their seats, which actually meant they had to get off and wait for another bus with empty seats.

Three of the people sitting in the same row as Rosa moved and gave up their seats. Rosa did not. When the bus driver demanded she give up her seat, she replied, 'I don't think I should have to stand up.' The bus driver contacted the police and she was arrested, which led to the black community boycotting the Montgomery bus system for over a year in protest. Eventually the United States District Court overturned these racial segregation laws. The catalyst was a 42-year-old seamstress who had the conviction of her beliefs. Not only did she publish her autobiography. *Rosa Parks: My Story,* she became a symbol for people around the world because of her courage and conviction.

To be able to stand up for what we believe in we need to be aware of our values and refer to them as we come across new situations, experiences and opportunities. More importantly, we need to listen to our inner vision to demonstrate our convictions through action.

Chapter 3

Who You Stand With – Your tribe

Who do you stand with? In simple terms, who has your back when needed and who cares about you? How much can you count on them? How much can they count on you?

Most of us surround ourselves with a group of friends and family we share our lives with. We feel a sense of connection and closeness, similar to that of a tribe.

For Native Americans a tribe was much more than a label for a group of people who lived and breathed similar values and worked together to keep their relationships in balance. This did not mean there were no arguments, but the tribe created a stronger sense of connection that pulled people together. It was an extension of a bloodline and the members of the tribe felt a sense of duty to protect and preserve one another. They also felt a sense of responsibility to pass their wisdom on to others within the tribe and teach them the ways of life.

The world we live in also has modern-day tribes. It may be a family tribe, a school tribe or a sporting tribe. Each of these may provide us with a strong sense of connection and security.

I believe the nature of these tribes has also shifted. In the past we were limited to physical and geographical boundaries, whereas we can now connect with members in other parts of the globe.

The number of contact touchpoints has also shifted over time. In the past, tribes had many gatherings and people would spend time together outside of these tribal gatherings. When I played sport at school, we would have practice four nights a week, with a game on the weekend. Now we belong to more tribes, so our time is spread across them and we have fewer touchpoints. I do not think that this is either good or bad, it is just a shift brought about by technology and increased exposure to new tribes.

Getting out of balance and off path has an impact on our tribes. When we get too busy, we often overlook the need to reconnect with our tribe, our family, friends and community. We forget to give back when others need us and stand with them.

Family

Families are significantly different now. Forty years ago, society had a specific guideline for what constituted a traditional family unit – a father, a mother and children. The extended family included the grandparents, siblings, aunts and uncles and cousins and most were located in close geographical proximity to the family unit.

That has changed. According to the United Nations Statistical Division (UNSTAT), the US divorce rate in 2011 was 53% and the Australian divorce rate 43%. This, of course, does not take into account the number of people who live together without an official marriage certificate. Because of this increase in marriage breakdown, there are more blended and extended families and more shuttling of children between divorced parents. I have come across no solid research or evidence that points to these trends being either good or bad for people or society.

However, this need to transport children from one home to another on a weekly or fortnightly basis, has made these families busier. Parents run from work to their evening activities but also have to taxi their children between sporting events and extracurricular activities. This pace has led to a stronger sense of busyness for families. Gone are the days of the family ritual of eating dinner together every night. People are coming and going so much they grab a meal when they can.

I believe we need to make a conscious effort to show our families they are important, to stop being so preoccupied with other priorities and take the time to stop and let our children know how important they are. We need more time together, more hugs and more real experiences. This can be easier if you listen to your inner vision, which lets you know that you need to show up more. Sometimes we also need a little reminder and here are a few ideas to get us started. Feel free to add to this list:

- Go for a walk with a family member and hold their hand.
- Surprise your spouse or partner with something you know they will appreciate (think back to the things you used to do for them when you first started dating and have not done in a long time).

- Take the time to look at your children when they tell you about their day at school – rather than continuing to cook dinner and pretending to listen.
- Make the extra effort to attend a school event that occurs during the day. (Yes – take an hour off work to show them that you care.)
- Have one of your children teach you something they have learnt.
- Call your parent and let them know a moment in time that they really made a difference in your life.
- Ask your parent for advice and thank them for giving it to you.
- Do something for a member of your extended family who needs a helping hand (offer before they ask you!).
- Ask a grandparent or older relative to tell you a story from their life – when they met their first love, what their first job was like, what they think about life.
- Spend time with an older relative who may need someone to share time and a meal with them.

Friends

Contrary to what Facebook would like us to believe, our friends are not just people in cyberspace. True friends are more than people posting photos of their dinner or ranting about their political views.

Friends are those we have developed a strong bond with. We know they have our backs and they know we have theirs. This is not just based on talk and false promises, our true friends have provided us with the meaning that shaped our lives through shared experiences. We often share our highest joys and our deepest fears with them – in words or actions.

We are not afraid to show them our true selves. We allow them to see us at our worst because we know they will accept us for who we are regardless. When we have friends who really know us, our true identity shines through.

How do you know if you have a true friend? If you called them with something important, would they shift their focus to you? If one of them needed your help, would you change your plans and give them your support? These are the common things that friends do for each other. The testing experiences that we share with them in life are what strengthens the bond of friendship. It makes it difficult to break.

We do not have to talk or touch base with our true friends on a daily or even regular basis. Have you ever had a really good friend you have not spoken to in a number of years? When you spend some time together or speak to them on the phone, it is as if you have never been apart.

Moving halfway across the world from the United States to Australia provided me with the next path to travel. Of course, geographical distance makes it more challenging to spend time with friends (although Skype and Google Hangouts makes it easier to see them!). Von is one of my best friends from high school. Two years can pass without us talking, however when we do it is as if we spoke last week. Although he lives on the other side of the world, I know we will always support each other.

The African Zulus have a saying for the greeting that occurs between two friends. When a Zulu tribe member comes across another, they stop and look at each other to take in their entire being and say, 'Sawabona' ('I see you'). This means they are present and giving their entire spirit and focus. The other Zulu responds with 'Sikhona' ('I am seen'), to show that they acknowledge and respect the connection that has just occurred. It is believed this may have been influenced by one of the most famous lines in James Cameron's blockbuster film film *Avatar.*

Community

I firmly believe that we need people to stand up more in their communities – to get actively involved to shape the type of community we want to live in. Too often people complain about everything they see going on in their community, but do nothing to create the change they regard as possible.

We can also be members of different communities or tribes. In my life I have a number of tribes I am a member of: my family tribe, my work tribe, my Thought Leader tribe, my school parents' tribe, my surf lifesaving tribe, my Hands Across the Water charity tribe and my soccer tribe.

All of these tribes gather for different purposes. However, by being involved with them I find a great sense of connection and fulfilment in the community around me. Although many of these people are more acquaintances than friends, because we are connected, we look out for one another.

I still enjoy playing soccer. I have to admit I am not a great player, but my soccer team accepts me as part of the tribe. During the soccer season, we play a game together every Saturday. We may see each other once during the week for a bit of practice and even though we do not commit to spending hours together during our normal week or in the off-season, if one of our tribe needs a hand they will put out a call and we help them.

These tribes show who we are as a person. They tell others what is important to us. More importantly, they stand with us when we need them and our lives are better for it.

Chapter 4

How You Live – Your actions and concentric rings

If a film crew followed you around for a full month, what would the footage show? Would it show you had lived in a way you would be proud of? Would the behaviours, interactions and actions you took demonstrate the beliefs and values you hold true?

How we live brings into reality who we are, what we stand for and who we stand with. Just as we leave our footprints on the ground, the way we live shows the footprints of our soul. This is why we need to stay true to our path. Without us living the life that we are meant to live, we are destined to continue walking in circles and having a deep thirst we cannot quench, no matter how many jobs we have, people we meet or experiences we face.

We have a choice to make: to follow our inner vision or not. I believe that life often has a way of reminding us from time to time if we are getting our Sacred Order right. Sometimes it is a pleasant reminder and at other times it can shake us to our very core and rock our world.

Often the way we live is for us and often it is for others. The way we live can send off powerful concentric rings that impact others around us. They can provide support when others need it but they can also turn people off. The energy behind these concentric rings often determines what type of impact we have.

Have you every walked down the street and smiled at a stranger walking in the opposite direction? The energy will often be reciprocated and they smile back. This is the impact of concentric rings.

Three types of concentric rings

There are different types of concentric rings. I often see these in the workplace, and I also see them in public or in schools. When I was a graduate student at Central Michigan University, I used to teach a course in Public Speaking. It was a mandatory class. Some of my class of about 35 students wanted to be there, many of them did not.

I gave them an assignment on the dynamics of non-verbal communication. They were to observe and study the messages they could see around them that did not involve the use of words or language. Their task was to explain what they saw by reading the responses other people had to some stimulus, such as a car, a person on a bicycle or someone communicating with another.

A few of my students decided to take this experiment a bit further and assess the other university lecturers. Every door to the classrooms had a window in it, so if you were late to a lecture, you could look through the window to determine a good time to walk in and find a seat. My students decided to use the window to assess the non-verbal body language of the students who were attending the lecture (which I am sure the dean would not have been too keen about).

When they reported back, they described having found three distinct groups. The majority of students were almost asleep – many of them looked bored. The second thing they noticed were a few students who looked annoyed and angry at what the lecturer was saying – some would roll their eyes and look at the student sitting next to them with disdain. The third group was smaller but displayed a different approach – they seemed to be on the edge of their seats, listening, with eyes wide open and their whole being tuned in to what the lecturer was saying.

Concentric Rings

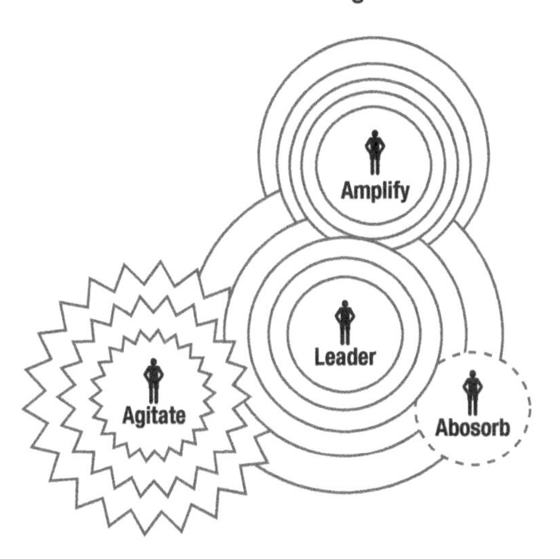

They were describing the three types of concentric rings. We impact other people in one of these three ways: Absorb, Agitate or Amplify.

Absorb

When you come into contact with another person and they appear to 'physically tune out' by looking busy or pretending not to notice, they are absorbing the concentric rings. This means that any message will be lost because they are not interested. It may be that the person delivering the message is not respected or have not done anything to earn your trust or attention. The energy and potential that could be shared is lost.

Agitate

When someone has rubbed someone else up the wrong way, this often creates concentric rings that are agitated. It is like when a stone is dropped into a pond and there is another stone that causes the ripple in the water to hit against it and fall back onto itself. The energy between these people has turned negative and you can feel the tension. This can also send other people in the vicinity running for cover to avoid getting sucked into this negative ball of energy. People will often agitate onto others, spreading this negativity.

Amplify

When a concentric ring truly connects with another person the impact is amplified, as if they have received a jolt of energy from the experience. This can be truly powerful because you can feel the tide of energy shift between people and grow in a positive way.

How you live and the concentric rings you give off make an impression on the world around you. They make our dent in the universe. We need more people to start stepping up and living the life they are meant to. We need more amplifiers who inspire others to walk their path and do the thing they know they should be doing.

At a higher level, if we can get people to focus on work and on their life, we can start creating a better world. When people get clearer on their critical path, we will start to see the amazing potential they have to make a real difference in the world.

Practical Exercise.

Who are you? Capture your external identity. Does this serve you? If not what do you need to change?

What do you stand for? What are the five to seven values you hold true and live your life by? When was the last time you stood up for something you believed in with conviction?

Are you giving to your tribe or taking from your tribe? When was the last time you did something unique for your family? For your friends?

What is something you know you should do in one of your community tribes? Is anything being lost from your lack of commitment?

What concentric rings are you sharing with others (absorb, agitate or amplify)?

Specific Life Critical Pathways

As in the business section of this book, I want to provide you with some examples of how you can map out your order or sequence to allow you to start progressing toward your critical path.

Although the specific details are always different, depending on the situation and people involved, there are a number of critical pathways I have found to be useful for many people.

In mapping these critical pathways, I have noticed there are usually five to seven milestones or touchpoints that comprise the higher order of what to do. The details and specifics generally fill out around this framework and make it easier to see and act on.

Here are a few examples of what the order looks like and a brief description of how to go about doing the right things, at the right time, in the right way. Please feel free to adapt this to assist you in standing up and demonstrating what you believe in and improving the concentric rings between you and members of your tribe.

Example 1: The critical path to increase quality time with family

One of the biggest challenges that working parents have is to increase the quality time they have with their families. The demands of work can make it tricky to balance work and home life.

Critical Path to Increasing Quality Time with Family

Order	Focus
1	Commit to family time
2	Schedule the time—block out tribe time
3	Do real things that have meaning
4	Follow up afterwards and thank them
5	Grab spontaneous unplanned time

The important thing is to track the signs of your interactions with your family. What would the concentric rings of the past week say to them? Would they have showed them they are important to you? Or something else? Regardless, it is critical to invest time and energy into both work and family and find a way to walk in both worlds.

Step 1: Commit to Family Time – Tribe time

The first step is to commit to having designated family time. If we do not separate the two worlds, it is generally time with family that suffers. We justify that by thinking without work and the income it brings in, the family would suffer. This is not really the truth. We often use this excuse to justify our behaviour in an attempt to reduce our guilt for not spending as much time with our family as we would like to.

Take the time to stand with the people that mean the most to you. Schedule a weekly or fortnightly date night with your spouse or partner. Make this the time when you reconnect with them and share some quality time having real conversations and rekindling the emotional bond you share. It is no wonder the divorce rate is around half, because couples do not take the time to connect and remind themselves of how wonderful they feel when they are together without the stress of everyday life.

If you have kids, do not let the weeks and months slip silently by and then realise they have gone. Too many parents wish they had made a bigger effort to spend quality time with their children. When I had young children and was working many hours to bring in the necessary income, I was thinking about my plan to retire early by working smarter. The only challenge was I would have to put in very long hours and weeks that involved travel overseas. A friend gave me some very sound advice: you can work harder and retire five to ten years earlier and have the money and financial security, or you can spend those five to ten years focused on your children, being there for the important events in their lives and helping them learn about life. In the long run, which is most important? Needless to say, I made the commitment to be in my children's lives much more (and found a way to make the income work too!).

To show conviction, tell others about this new commitment. Talk to your family about how much you enjoy spending time with them and how you would like to find a way to have a couple of hours a week just for them. If you want to take it a step further, tell your work colleagues and friends what you are committing to. This network usually is more interested in you and will often follow up with you to check in and see how it is going. Also, if they want to spend time with you, they also know the family commitment you have and will respect it enough to find another time to be with you.

Step 2: Schedule the Time – Block out

Make a personal commitment to focus on scheduling time with your family. If you do not schedule time in your diary, it will get taken up by something unplanned. The goal is to consciously commit the time and make it a habit or routine.

Weekly tribe time

I know a number of people who will block out a certain amount of time each week and coordinate it with school, sport and other activities. This becomes a consistent goal each week, to have what I call Tribe Time. Labelling it makes it something more important that just hanging out – it makes it sacred. When things are sacred they are valued and people respect them more. In fact, many workplaces, schools and religions have rituals that create a strong shared meaning for the people taking part. Think of when school children sing the national anthem, or companies have a presentation to the employee of the month. By creating your own Tribe Time ritual, you can commit to allocating time to share experiences with your family.

Tribe retreats

It is also important to plan for family time away from the normal environment. We grow even more when we come into contact and experience different cultures and places. Whether it is visiting another country where you don't speak the language, driving across the state to a place you have never been or staying in a hotel in the city you live in, it all helps broaden our perspective.

We camp together as a family every Easter long weekend. We gather all the tents and sleeping bags and head to our annual spot right near the ocean. The kids love it as they get to run around on the beach, walk on the trails and get back to nature (and I am sure they enjoy not having to shower every day!). We have created our own rituals for this annual retreat. We always make a fire at least one evening (often using a bow drill to rub sticks together to make the fire) and roast marshmallows. We have a great Easter egg hunt where the adults hide the chocolate eggs and the kids run around looking for them. We follow this up with a huge family and friends soccer match. The kids look forward to these rituals every year and I know that when they return to school they talk about these activities with a sense of pride and connection.

Tribe Retreats provide shared meanings for you and your family – moments in time that will be remembered and cherished for years to come. They are full of unexpected things that take us by surprise and stretch us. Can you remember a time when it was late and you needed to find a place to stay which challenged everyone, but the next day the family found the pool and spent most of the day playing together laughing and having water fights? Or when you found a wonderful restaurant that had a breakfast buffet the kids raved about – and you had to drag them away because they were so excited about it? This is good medicine for the heart and the soul.

Step 3: Do Real Things– Meaning

When your family tribe comes together, make it mean something. Don't just allow the kids to jump on their iPads while you keep glancing at your email inbox to catch up. This will not work because it is typical time, not special time.

We need to do things that will provide meaning for them. This can be anything as long as it is a shared experience, such as spending time putting together a puzzle or playing a board game or cards. The kids just want to spend time playing with you. This is about having fun and taking the time to have fun with them – so do it.

There are a range of activities you can do that will provide these experiences and shared family meanings. Do real things that will provide a lasting memory. You do not have to spend a lot of money although sometimes you will because it can open doors to additional experiences to share together. Some family activities could include:

- Go on a walk and ask them what the best part of their day has been and why.
- Paint a picture together on canvas (or paper).
- Play a game outside that everyone can participate in.
- Go on a walking tour of your city and learn about its history.
- Collect leaves from trees and see who can find the biggest (older kids can identify the type of tree).
- Take them to a park and go exploring for wildlife. Have a competition to see who can spot the greatest number of bird species.
- Take them to a sporting event that you can watch together and cheer for your home team.
- Build a fort (inside or out) that you can physically go into and play.

Make your time together count. Focus your entire being on your family. This will let them know that you are there for them. This time to play, connect and share experiences is what shapes young minds. Make it mean something.

Step 4: Follow up Afterwards– Thank them

Regardless of what activity you do with your family, thank them afterwards. Give them a hug to let them know you appreciate them and you loved the time you just spent with them. These concentric rings are extremely powerful – they provide a physical anchor or reminder of the event in their mind. Saying thank you is good, but a warm hug takes it to the next level.

I also recommend that a couple of days later you go back over the event in your mind. Think about what it was that touched your soul and theirs and reflect on it. Share it with them a couple of days later, letting them know you valued the time and are looking forward to the next Tribe Time. When you say this, take a look at the expression on their faces. If it was something that they really enjoyed you will be able to see it, and they will relive the positive feeling they had during the event.

Step 5: Grab Spontaneous Time – Unplanned

Look for moments of spontaneous time you and your family can grab. It is often unplanned events that give you a chance to have Tribe Time you had not expected. This is a bonus and you should grab it with both hands and jump in.

I find this time is often there, you just need to look for it. It can be when you are getting ready for work in the morning and have a spare 30 minutes (hard to imagine, but it does happen). You could fix a nice breakfast for your spouse or partner to have together before you both rush off to work. It may be when you realise you have a couple of hours in the afternoon that you can get out of work and grab the kids to spend some time playing with them. Pick them up from school and let them know you are calling a spontaneous Tribe Time and go on an adventure. Grab some ice-cream and make it a game where they need to talk about one interesting or good thing that happened to them during their day. Pick from the list above or chose your own activity.

If people took the time to get their order right at home with their loved ones as much as they focused at work, we would have happier partners and families. By increasing your awareness and commitment to family time you can make a positive difference to them, and be more fulfilled yourself.

Example 2: The critical path to helping kids with homework

If you have children at school, you will have experienced the joys of homework. For children around the world this is a normal assignment to help enhance their learning. I can remember doing homework and thinking how happy I would be when I had a job and did not have to do homework again. If I only I had known that homework continues throughout life.

Critical Path to Helping Kids with Homework

Order	Focus
1	Show interest in their homework
2	Look at assignment objectives
3	Ask them what they think—map on paper
4	Provide ideas—not the end result
5	Proofread, suggest and recognise effort

One of the challenges with helping kids with their schoolwork is that, for many adults, it may be 20 years since they learnt what the kids are being taught. Our memories may not be what they used to be and this can create a few issues. Many kids expect their parents to know everything. It makes sense, we finished school years ago and the kids assume that we studied the same things.

There is a critical path that can be followed by anyone who has been frustrated by the challenge of how to help their children learn.

Step 1: Show interest in their homework

The most important step to start with is to show you are interested in their homework. Remember what it was like to be a child? Remember when you learnt new things and this opened up a whole new exciting world to you? When you were passionate about learning something, did you want to wait – or were you so enthusiastic that it was hard to contain yourself?

Kids are the same. If we do not take the time to recognize and appreciate that they have homework and want us to help them learn, then we are dampening their spirit. The last thing we want is to demotivate them around learning and homework.

So when they let you know they have homework, show interest. Ask them if you can work on it together as you want to see what they are learning.

Step 2: Look at assignment objectives

Given it may have been a few decades since you last learnt the same subject matter, be careful not to assume that you know the answers to what is being asked. I made this mistake with my eldest daughter on one of her math assignments only to have her bring it home the next day covered in red ink because most of it was wrong (not a good time, but definitely a learning experience and a mistake I will not make again!).

Read through the assignment before starting to help answer the questions. Ask your child what they have been doing in class to help you understand the frameworks and concepts the teacher has been trying to get across. Most homework is sequential, which means the class and the teacher discuss some of the theories and models and do a few practice exercises before the teacher sets it as work to be completed at home. Get an overview of the purpose of the assignment, which may be more important.

Step 3: Ask them what they think – map on paper

The temptation with helping your children with their homework is to take over and do it for them. Of course it is much easier and quicker for you to do this, but it is not your homework! This takes away the learning and deeper understanding that your child needs.

Start by asking them what they think the possible ways are that they can do the homework. If necessary, use a blank sheet of paper and map out their ideas to help keep it separate from the linear homework questions that are often provided. By mapping the ideas on another piece of paper you can both see what you are discussing, which makes it easier for them to understand. Some helpful questions to ask include:

- How do you think you should complete the homework (in their head, in the book, on paper, on a computer, etc.)?
- What do you think the teacher is looking for? What will the end result look like?
- What have you been learning in class that you may be able to use to help you complete this assignment?

Once you have started with how to complete the homework, then start looking at the specific assignment and questions being asked. Draw out their thoughts so you can understand what they are comprehending. It can also be useful to have them put their thoughts down on a sheet of paper to help them reflect on what it is that they are thinking about.

Step 4: Provide ideas – not end result

As you work through the homework questions, do not be tempted to tell them the answer. A big part of learning is using a problem-solving process to arrive at an answer. If you just give them the end result, they will miss this vital learning process.

Instead, provide them with ideas and questions that will lead them to discover the answer. Once they have started to formulate their final answer, continue their learning by asking them why or how they arrived at this answer. Remember, the goal is to have them learn and to allow them to come up with the answer or end result themselves – not you providing it for them.

I also find it is useful to give them metaphors or other examples they can relate to that are similar to what the homework is asking. For example, if they are learning about simple math and fractions, help them to see what it is in a practical way. Take an apple and slice it up into quarters so they can see what fractions look like. Use this to provide ideas on taking concepts that are two-dimensional into real life.

Step 5: Proofread, suggest and recognize for effort

Once they have completed their assignment, take the time to proofread and provide suggestions. Be careful not to just point out what is wrong. This is not the best way to encourage learning, which requires trial and error and making mistakes. If they have done something incorrectly, ask them to take another look at it. Or ask them to show you the process they used to come up with the answer. Often they were in a hurry, or they just missed a step, and this led to the wrong result.

Another important thing to do is to recognize the effort they are putting in. Once they have completed a couple of tasks, let them know you are proud of them for concentrating and getting that far. Give them encouragement to complete the rest of the homework.

I also recommend that, when it is completed, you find a way to give them a reward. It does not have to be something big like $50 or a new bike, but it should be something that demonstrates you are proud of them. It can be as simple as making a chocolate milkshake or giving them a snack or piece of candy. Often, just giving them a big hug and telling them that you are proud of them, will be all they need to look forward to the next time you help them with their homework.

By taking a few minutes to get our order and sequence right, we can make it much easier for our children to learn and complete their homework in a positive way. Who knows, you may even relearn some of the things you have forgotten from when you were in school!

Chapter 5

Fast Track Tables of Critical Paths for Life

To provide you with a further reference, I wanted to share with you a table of useful critical paths in life. Please feel free to modify and adapt these to further enhance your situation.

Critical Path to being financially free
Critical Path to successful date nite
Critical Path to getting kids to clean up their room
Critical Path to proposing marriage
Critical Path to teaching a child a skill
Critical Path to volunteering for a charity
Critical Path to writing a book

Note: Each of these Paths will have 5 steps that will be listed to show the order to be followed.

Critical Path to being financially free

Order	Focus
1	Identify your freedom target
2	Don't waste money (budget/spending)
3	Find ways to make more income
4	Find Leverage (property/business/shares)
5	Monitor and modify over time

Critical Path to successful date nite

Order	Focus
1	Choose the date type: meal/activity/event
2	Pick a date that works and lock it in
3	Organise someone to look after the kids
4	Find something unique to add to the date (flowers, candy, gift, etc)
5	Remind spouse/partner and reconfirm logistics

Critical Path to getting kids to clean up their room

Order	Focus
1	Identify what will motivate them to clean up room
2	Share with them why room needs to be cleaned up and ask for their help using identified motivation
3	Clean the room together to show desired end result
4	Provide a timeframe and get them to commit—with consequences if necessary
5	Recognise and praise for efforts or find out why they did not do and reconsider motivation or consequences

Critical Path to proposing marriage

Order	Focus
1	Identify what they would want (traditional or unique approach—meal/activity/event)
2	Select the date and place to propose
3	Identify what you will do in what order
4	Organise location or assistance from others
5	Identify and organise memento of the event (engagement ring, photo, gift, etc)

Critical Path to teaching a child a skill

Order	Focus
1	Identify what skills they want to learn and why
2	Map out the components or steps of the skill
3	Show them how to do the skill (step by step)
4	Have them practice and guide them as needed
5	Recognise and praise for effort

Critical Path to volunteering for a charity

Order	Focus
1	Identify a charity that you admire
2	Identify something the charity does that you would like to get involved in
3	Identify what skills or assistance you can provide
4	Identify the time that you have available to donate
5	Contact the charity and volunteer

Critical Path to writing a book

Order	Focus
1	Identify purpose, topic, title
2	Identify main points and order
3	Gather research to support
4	Write content, add stories and pictures
5	Edit and publish

Final Words

So what is the next step? What is your inner vision telling you to take action on? Listen to it. Share it. Act on it. Live it. Make the world a better place for today and the future.

If you are a leader in business, shift your order to ensure that you are creating a workplace that is a source of connection, growth and fulfillment. If you are a staff member, step up and lead others when they need someone to follow and encourage those around you to do the same.

In your home life, take time to connect with the loved ones who, too often, we take for granted. Show them you care for them and that they are important to you. If you are lucky enough to have children, take time to give them that little bit of extra attention the next time you see them. They will carry your legacy into the future. Make sure that it is one filled with optimism, hope and belief in what can be accomplished.

My wish for you is that you have the conviction to follow what you know to be your truth. That you walk with courage down the path you are meant to be on. And that your concentric rings create a positive ripple extending to the people around you and beyond.

Stay True to Your Path.

References and Recommended Reading

Ail on: *Five Steps to a Strategic Plan*, Forbes, July 2015

Aldama, Zigor: *Inside the Chinese Boot Camp Treating Internet Addiction*, Telegraph Media Group, January 2015

Allen, David: *Getting Things Done: The art of stress-free productivity*, Penguin Books, 2015

Angell, Marcia: *The Epidemic of Mental Illness: Why?*, *New York Review of Books*, June 2011

Australian Government, Australian Institute of Health and Welfare: *Overweight and Obesity*

Barbe, Walter, Swassing. Raymond, Milone, Michael: *Teaching Through Modality Strengths: Concepts and practices*, Zaner-Bloser Inc. 1979

Bean, Daryl: *Journal of Personality and Social Psychology*, Cornell University, 2011

Bem, Daryl J: 'Feeling the Future: Experimental evidence for anomalous retroactive influences on cognition and affect', American Psychological Association, Cornell University, 2011

Brown, Tom Jr.: *The Science and Art of Tracking*, The Berkley Publishing Group, 1999

Brown, Tom Jr.: *The Tracker*, The Berkley Publishing Group, 1978

Buzan, Tony: *Use your Head: Innovative learning and thinking, the power of creative intelligence and how to mind map* BBC Active, Educational Publishers, 1996

Cabral, M & Bornemann, T & Levav, I: 'Mental Health: A Call for Action', World Health Organisation, 2000

Canfield, J & Hansen, M V & Hewitt, L: *The Power of Focus: How to hit your business, personal and financial targets with confidence and certainty*, Vermillion, August 2013

Carr, Nicholas: *The Shallows: How the internet is changing the way we think, read and remember*, Atlantic Books, 2010

Carr, Nicholas: 'Automation Makes Us Dumb', *The Wall Street Journal*, November 2014

Chua, Amy: *Battle Hymn of the Tiger Mother*, Bloomsbury Publishing, 2012

Chui, Michael & Manyika, James & Bughin, Jacques & Dobbs, Richard & Roxburgh, Charles & Sarrazin, Hugo & Sands, Geoffery & Westergreen, Magdalena: 'The Social Economy; Unlocking Value and Productivity through Social Technologies', McKinsey Global Institute, July 2012

Church, Matt: *Amplifiers: The power of motivational leadership to inspire and influence*, John Wiley & Sons Australia Ltd, 2013

Clemons, Rachel: 'Milk Buying Guide', *Choice*, August 2014

Co-op: '2015 Future Leaders Index White Paper 1', BDO, 2015

Co-op: '2015 Future Leaders Index White Paper 2', BDO, 2015

Collins, Jim: *Good to Great: Why some companies make the leap and others don't*, HarperCollins*Publishers*, 2000

Conner, Cheryl: *Employees Really Do Waste Time at Work*, Forbes, July 2012

Conner, Cheryl: 'Who Wastes the Most Time at Work?', *Forbes Magazine*, September 2013

Cook, Peter: *The New Rules of Management: How to revolutionise productivity, innovation and engagement by implementing projects that matter*, John Wiley & Sons Australia Ltd, 2013

Dawley, Heidi: 'Time-wise, internet is now TV's equal', *Medialife Magazine*, January 2006

Duhigg, Charles: *The Power of Habit: Why we do what we do in life and business*, Random House Publishing Group, February 2012

Dweck, Carol: *Mindset: The new psychology of success*, Ballantine Books, 2006

Eyal, Nir: *Hooked: How to build habit forming products*, Penguin Books, 2014

Ferriss, Tim: *The 4-Hour Workweek*, Crown Publishing Group, 2007

Folk, James: 'Digital Detox: How taking a break from technology can help you reclaim your life, reduce stress and achieve success.' 2014

Fox, Jason: *The Game Changer: How to use the science of motivation with the power of game design to shift behaviour, shape culture and make clever happen*, Wrightbooks, 2014

Fried, Jason, and Heinemeier, H: *Rework*, Crown Business, 2010

Friedman, Thomas: *The World is Flat*, Farrar, Straus and Giroux, 2005

Goodin, Seth: *Tribes*, Hachette Digital, 2008

Goertzel, Ben: 'Is Precognition Real', Cornell University, *HP Plus Magazine*, November 2012

Goleman, Daniel: *The Hidden Driver of Excellence*, HarperCollins*Publishers*, 2013

Gouvei, Aaron: '2014 Wasting Time at Work Survey', Salary.com, 2014

Greene, Robert: *Mastery*, Penguin Books, 2012

Halford, Scott: *Activate Your Brain: How understanding your brain can improve your work and your life*. Greanleaf Book Group Press, 2015

Harnois, Gaston & Gabriel, Phyllis: 'Mental Health Work: Impact, Issues and Good Practices', Digital Commons, Cornell University, 2000

Henderson, Michael: 'Get Tribal: Simple, sound advice for understanding and improving your workplace culture', Cultures at Work, 2011

Howard, Gardner Prof: *Frames of Mind: The theory of multiple intelligences*, Basic Books, 1993

Hsin, Amy & Xie, Yu: 'Asians Outperform White Students because they try harder, study finds', Phys Org, May 2014

Hunt-Davis, Ben: *Will It Make the Boat Go Faster?*, Matador, 2011

Investopedia: '*The Causes and Costs of Absenteeism in the Workplace*', *Forbes Magazine*, July 2013

Khan, Salman: *The One World Schoolhouse: Education reimagined*, Twelve Books Hatchette Publishing, 2012

Kreider, Tim: 'The 'Busy' Trap', *New York Times*, June 2012

Lavinksy, Dave: 'Pareto Principle: How To Use It To Dramatically Grow Your Business', *Forbes Magazine*, January 2014

Leiner, Barry M & Cerf, Vinton G & Clark, David D & Kahn, Robert E & Kleinrock, Leonard & Lynch, Daniel C & Postel, Jon & Roberts, Larry G & Wolff, Stephen: 'Brief History of the Internet', Internet Society

Levitin, Daniel: *The Organised Mind: Thinking straight in the age of information overload*, Penguin Group, July 2015

Linker, Josh: '*The 21 Most Creative Job Titles*', Forbes, 2014

Lipman, Victor: '*Surprising, Disturbing Facts from the Mother of all Employee Engagement Surveys*', Forbes, September 2013

Lott Jr, Dr John R: 'Is gun ownership really down in America?', Fox News, March 2015

Lott, John R & Whitely, John E & Riley, Rebekah C: 'Concealed Carry Permit Holders Across the United States', Crime Prevention Research Centre, July 2014

Marshall, Perry: '80/20 Sales and Marketing – The Definitive Guid to Working Less and Making More' Entrepreneur Press, January 2013

Mayo Clinic Staff: 'Chronic Stress puts your health at risk', Mayo Clinic, July 2013

Medibank Private: 'The Cost of Workplace Stress in Australia', August 2008

Merton, Robert: *Social Theory and Social Structure*, The Free Press, 1968

Mossbridge, J & Tressoldi, P & Utts, J: 'Predictive physiological anticipation preceding seemingly unpredictable stimuli: a meta-analysis', *Frontiers in Psychology*, October 2012

Park, Alice: 'The Tiger Mom Effect is Real', *Time Magazine*, May 2014

Parks, Rosa: *Rosa Parks: My Story*, Puffin Books, 1992

Porras, Jerry I & Collins, Jim: 'Built to Last – Successful Habits of Visionary Companys' William Collins, October 1994

Pressman, Aaron: 'Candy Crush: So popular it's killing king's IPO?', Yahoo Finance, December 2013

Radicati, Sara: 'Email Statistics Report 2014-2018', The Radicati Group, Inc, April 2014

Safe Work Australia: 'Mental Stress costs Australian businesses more than $10 billion per year', April 2013

Safe Work Australia: 'The incidence of accepted workers' compensation claims for mental stress in Australia', April 2013

Sander, Peter: *What Would Steve Jobs Do?*, McGraw Hills, 2012

Schwartz, B: *The Paradox of Choice: Why more is less*, HarperCollins*Publishers*, 2014

Seligman, Martin Dr: *Learned Optimism*, Random House Australia, 2011

Skok, David: 'Lessons Learned – Viral Marketing', Entrepreneurs.com, December 2009

Stafford, Tom: 'Psychology: Why bad news dominates the headlines', BBC Future, July 2015

Sunshine, James: 'Workers spend one-fourth of workday reading, responding to email Survey', *Huffington Post*, January 2012

Taylor, Frederick: *The Principles of Scientific Management*, Harper and Brothers, 1911

Thompson, John & McKeay, Martin & Brenner, Bill & Möller, Richard & Sintorn, Mathias & Huston, Geoff: 'Akamai's State of the Internet Report', Akamai Technologies, 2014

Trussler, Marc & Soroka, Stuart: 'Consumer Demand for Cynical and Negative News Frames', *The International Journal of Press/Politics*, Sage Publications, March 2015

WHO: '*Global burden of mental disorders and the need for comprehensive, coordinated response from health and social sectors at the country level*' World Health Organisation, December 2011

About the author

Scott Stein is known as the Pathfinder. He blends Native American heritage and philosophy into practical strategies that people can use at work and at home. Although his great grandmother was a full-blood Cherokee medicine woman, Scott did not learn the Cherokee ways and grew up in a typical suburban family in America. He has always been drawn to the wilderness and became an adventure guide, leading or participating in adventure trips across the United States, Canada, Europe, South America, Asia and Australia. He was fortunate to be taught by a teacher who had learnt the art of awareness, survival and philosophy from an Apache elder.

After receiving his Masters Degree, he taught Communication and Public Speaking at Central Michigan University. His role as a learning and development manager for five manufacturing plants gave him an opportunity to hone his practical business skills as he assisted in turning the enterprise around by improving the culture and lifting performance.

He has been based in Sydney, Australia, since 1995 as an owner of a national learning and development company and now travels the globe to help people identify and take action toward their critical path. As a consultant to many leading national and international businesses and organizations, Scott guides them in implementing strategies that inspire their leaders and their people to do the things that matter in the right order to achieve improved results.

He is a Thought Leader Global Partner and co-author of *Thought Leaders: How to capture, package and deliver your ideas for greater commercial success* and *Sell Your Thoughts: How to earn a million dollars a year as a Thought Leader.*

Scott believes in building community and giving back. He is a founding board member of Hands Across the Water, an Australian charity established after the 2004 Boxing Day Tsunami. It has raised almost $15million and cares for over 600 children across six orphanages and a community centre in Thailand. What makes the charity unique is that 100 per cent of donations goes directly to the projects without any donors funds being spent on administration, marketing or staff in Australia.

Here are a few things to help you on your path.

On Scott's website you will find a range of free resources and downloadable templates you can use to help you map your Critical Path. www.scottstein.com.au/resources

His free e-newsletter provides regular reminders and helpful tips and techniques you can use to help you at work and at home. Go to www.scottstein.com.au to sign up and start receiving wisdom beyond the book.

Scott also works with leaders and organizations to bring these strategies into reality. He provides a range of powerful insights, advice and programs including: Critical Path Leadership, Compression Planning Strategy and Thought Leadership Development.

If you are organizing a conference and want an incredible speaker who has a real message everyone can relate to, please contact Scott at scott@scottstein.com.au. He is known for his inspirational style that encourages people to get involved, stay on path and take action at work – and at home.